MASTER PAINTERS

VERMEER

THE COMPLETE WORKS

AGNESE ANTONINI

BARNES & NOBLE
NEW YORK

Contents

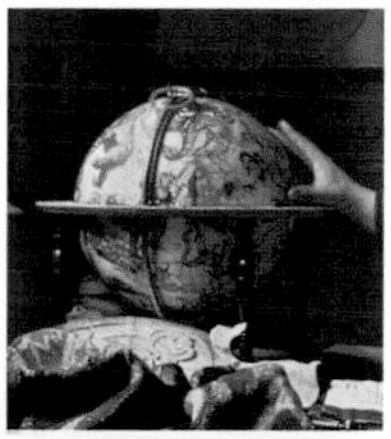

Chapter 1
The Sphinx of Delft

Vermeer has been called the Sphinx of Delft, a nickname attributed to Théophile Thoré-Bürger, and in many ways it sums up what we know of the Dutch artist's life and career. Much of his life is shrouded in mystery, and this sense of enigma has become a profoundly important part of how his work is understood. We do not know, for example, Vermeer's exact birthday; the event is noted only in his baptismal record a few days later. That document records the baptism of Joannis, or Johannes, as the artist himself would come to spell it, Vermeer on October 31, 1632, in the New Church in Delft, a Dutch town a few miles from The Hague. Situated in the middle of the town's main market square, the New Church was at the heart of Delft's Calvinist community, and it stood in contrast to the Old Church, where the city's Catholics worshipped.

Vermeer was born into a Protestant family, part of a community that had associated the struggle against Spanish political oppression with the corruption of the Catholic Church. Vermeer's parents, Reynier Janszoon (or Jansz) and Digna Balthasars (or Baltens), had a daughter, Gertruy, and then twelve years later their second child and only son was born. He was named for his grandfather Jan, a tailor, although his parents gave him the Latin version of that name. Last names were not common in seventeenth-century Holland, and Reynier was an adult when he acquired his. Johannes first chose Vos ("fox") and then Vermeer, and he continued to use both surnames throughout his life. When he acted as an innkeeper he signed himself Vos, but as an art dealer he preferred Vermeer.

Reynier was born in Antwerp in 1591 and moved to Amsterdam in 1611 to learn to be a silk weaver. He moved to Delft shortly after marrying Digna, and in about 1628 he rented an inn—it was called *De Vliegende Vos ("The Flying Fox")*—on the Voldersgracht, the canal that ran behind the market square. In about 1631 Reynier began a second career as an hotelier, although he continued, at least at first, to work as a weaver. Then on October 13, 1631, Reynier was admitted as an art dealer to the Guild of St. Luke, the painters' guild. It is quite possible that his decision to pursue yet another profession was linked to the inn, as inns were often used for buying and selling works of art. It is not clear how

Attributed to
Johannes Vermeer
The Procuress (detail)
1656, oil on canvas
4.7 x 4.3 ft. (143 x 130 cm)
Staatliche Kunstsammlungen,
Gemäldegalerie,
Dresden

long Reynier pursued all three careers—that of innkeeper, art dealer, and head of a silk workshop—but it seems likely that he had abandoned cloth manufacturing by 1645 because he is no longer identified as a weaver in any document after that date. Vermeer's father certainly must have developed an ability to draw as an apprentice silk weaver, and later, as an art dealer, he had frequent contact with collectors and artists, including painters like Balthasar van der Ast, who painted flowers, as well as Pieter van Steenwyck and Pieter Anthonisz van Groenewegen. Each of these artists may have exerted some influence over Vermeer's early stylistic development.

We have only one, indirect reference to Vermeer between the time of his baptism in 1632 and his marriage in 1653, and it comes in his father's will, executed by Willem de Langue on February 17, 1638. Any reconstruction of the artist's early life is thus based only on circumstantial evidence, and gaps remain

Balthasar van der Ast
Still Life with Fruit, Flowers, and Parrots
ca. 1620
Hermitage Museum, St. Petersburg

especially with regard to Vermeer's artistic training. There are documents, however, which record father Reynier's frequent contacts with the important artists of his day, especially still-life and landscape painters, and Reynier's relationships with the artists and collectors in Delft and The Hague offer a valuable source for understanding his son's early development. The quality of light present in some of those works would become characteristic of the paintings of Pieter de Hooch, Gerard Houckgeest, and Emanuel de Witte as well as those of Vermeer himself—it is this group of artists that made the school of Delft famous between 1650 and 1660.

Pieter van Steenwyck
Vanitas
Seventeenth century
Prado Museum,
Madrid

In the spring of 1641, when he was nine, young Johannes and his family moved from the *Flying Fox* to a big house attached to the inn and facing the large market square. It was called Mechelen after the family's native city in Flanders. His parents bought this house—they had rented the first one—and

Mechelen remained the artist's property even after he and his wife and children went to live in his mother-in-law's house. Like his father, Vermeer worked as an innkeeper and art dealer to supplement his income and support his family.

The war and later skirmishes that marked the second half of the sixteenth century in Holland had obvious consequences for the country's economy. The wars notwithstanding, Delft enjoyed a cultural and economic boom in the seventeenth century, the evidence for it apparent in the numerous commercial and craft ventures that thrived there at the time. The most important was the manufacturing of the famous blue-and-white ceramics that were exported throughout Europe, but the city also produced beer and tapestries. A number of Delft's successful workshops and commercial enterprises were run by women, and Vermeer's paternal grandmother, Neelthe Goris, was among the most energetic and entrepreneurial of them. Indeed, Vermeer's family was full of extravagant personalities, including Balthasar Claesz Gerrits, his maternal grandfather and a watchmaker, whose activities as a forger finally required the intervention of the Estates General and the governor.

Delft Pottery
Decorative Tiles
Seventeenth century
Museum of London

Guillaume Courtois
Battle of Luetzen
1656
Galleria Palatina,
Florence

As an important commercial center, Delft had a successful middle class that proved to be both interested in and able to acquire works of art. Delft's splendor, however, did not last; it ran the gamut, more or less, of Vermeer's career and was marked by the extraordinary relationship between that artist and his city. When Vermeer died Delft fell again into the provincial somnolence from which it had been awakened, fifty years earlier, by the intense wave of immigration brought on by a complex series of historical events.

The seventeenth century in the Low Countries opened as war raged between the northern, Protestant provinces and the Catholic armies of Philip II of Spain, who was determined to reassert his authority over the rebellious territories. Holland was one of the northern provinces that, in 1579, formed the Utrecht Union and declared independence from Spain under the banner of the Republic of the Seven United Provinces. And even though the Catholic minority in Holland allied itself with the Calvinist and Lutheran communities in a common struggle against Spanish oppression, the conflict in the Low Countries was enmeshed in the larger wars of religion that had, as a result of the Protestant Reformation, engulfed all of Europe in the middle of the sixteenth century. Delft was the favorite residence of the Spanish viceroy, or *Stadtholder*, William of Orange, known also as William the Silent, who was at the heart of the revolt against Philip II and to whom the city leaders swore an oath of allegiance in 1572. That act marked the city's transition from Catholic to Protestant domination, and from then on Delft played a crucial role in the newly formed league of Protestant cities in the northern provinces. Once the conflict ended the city became a symbol of national independence. William was killed in 1584, but the war against Spain continued. The Twelve Year Truce, signed in 1609, finally brought some easing of tensions, at least until 1621, and it allowed Holland a period of relative prosperity. The seven provinces of the northern Low Countries were successful in gaining independence from Spain, although official recognition of this status came later, with the final peace accords and the separation of Catholic Flanders. Fighting began again in 1621 and only ended with the Peace of Westphalia in 1648. That treaty marked the conclusion of the Thirty Years' War, a war that had actually begun in 1568, some eighty years earlier. Shortly afterward, however, the Low Countries were again forced to take to the battlefield, first against the English and then the French. In the years of the truce with Spain, Delft and indeed all of Holland had enjoyed tremendous economic prosperity. This was due in large part to the founding of two great commercial enterprises, the Dutch East Indies Company (1602) and then the Dutch West Indies Company (1621). In that brief span of time the United Provinces built the most powerful naval and merchant marine fleets in all of Europe. Dutch prosperity also attracted heavy immigration from Flanders, and this influx of people became the engine for a notable expansion in the population and the rapid growth of the cities.

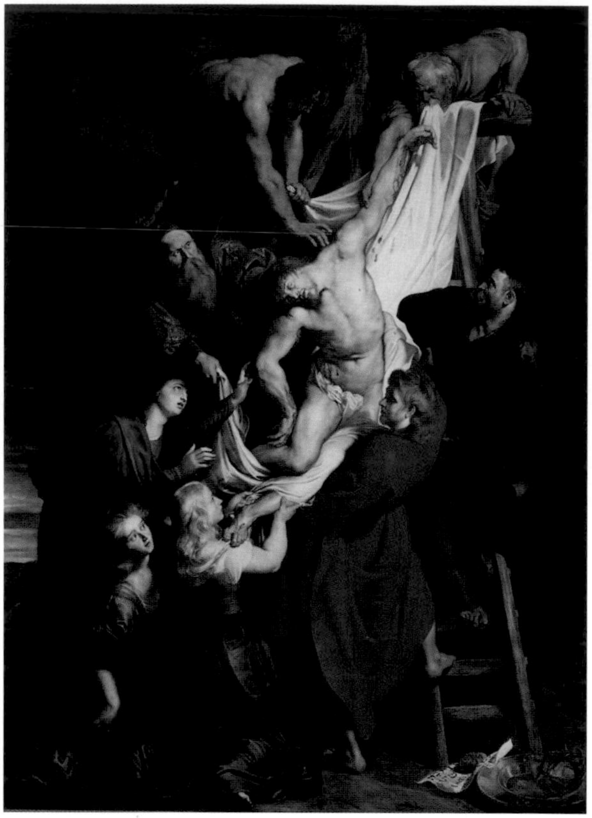

Peter Paul Rubens
Descent from the Cross
ca. 1612
Cathedral of Our Lady, Antwerp

Independence for the United Provinces, achieved for all intents and purposes in 1609, also set the regions of Flanders and the Low Countries on a different artistic course. While Flemish artists like Rubens, Van Dyck, and Jacob Jordaens contributed to the development and diffusion of the European baroque, painters in the Low Countries inherited the "realistic" tendencies that had distinguished Flemish painting since the fifteenth century. This is in part due to the fact that the northern provinces were Protestant and had very little aristocratic or ecclesiastical patronage. Calvinism also officially banned frescoes and pictures in churches. As a consequence Dutch painting was shaped by the desire of a class

Frans Francken II
The Antiquarian's Shop
ca. 1645
Galleria Borghese, Rome

of well-to-do people to decorate their own homes, and pictures with subject matters and dimensions appropriate to domestic interiors were especially popular. The careful distinction in this period between the different genres of painting—portraiture, landscapes, religious scenes, and still lifes—was also a response to the needs of a new clientele. Nor was it just the rich merchant families that collected art; artisans and shopkeepers also bought paintings. Yet despite the lively art market many artists pursued second careers to guarantee sufficient income to support themselves and their families, and they also began to specialize in different genres to satisfy the tastes of their new patrons. John Evelyn noted this in his dairy when he visited the annual fair in Rotterdam on August 31, 1641. He remarked on the enormous number of paintings for sale there: "We arrived late in Rotterdam when the annual market, or fair, was there. I was surprised at the number of pictures there, and especially landscapes and those comic scenes we call drolleries. The number of paintings and their modest prices can be explained by the lack of land in which to invest, and thus it is not unusual to find a simple farmer who has invested as much as two or three thousand pounds sterling in those goods." Nonetheless, patronage in this period was more varied than it might seem because a less rigorously enforced iconoclasm meant that the church had not completely stopped commissioning art. The figure of the art dealer also emerges in the seventeenth century; he was a collector or merchant who focused on a single artist, reserving the right to purchase the whole of his production, as was the case between Vermeer and Pieter Claesz van Ruijven. This aristocratic collector, according to some scholars, owned twenty-one of the artist's works, which were put up for sale in Amsterdam in 1696.

Gerard ter Borch
The Concert
1650s
Louvre Museum, Paris

Vermeer's early formation certainly must be considered within this context, but at the same time it is almost impossible to reconstruct the early part of his career. We know nothing of his training or with whom or where he apprenticed, leaving us to work only with circumstantial evidence and educated guesses. The young Johannes was likely in elementary school, where he would have learned to read and write, about 1641, and he also attended a small academy on the Voldersgracht where he was taught the rudiments of mathematics and drawing. Johannes Vermeer was admitted to the Guild of St. Luke on December 29, 1653, and we can assume that by then he had completed the six years of apprenticeship with a recognized master required by the guild. Membership in the guild, a professional organization that included a variety of professions and diverse specialties, was the indispensable condition in Holland for practicing the art of painting, and in return the institution promised to protect its members from those who practiced their profession illegally. (The names of the professional guilds preserved the memory of their patron saints; St. Luke was the patron saint of artists.) It is likely that Vermeer spent the first two years of his apprenticeship with a local master so that he could continue to live at home. He then would have gone to Utrecht or Amsterdam for the remaining four years of his training. Several artists have been identified as Vermeer's first master. Evert van Aelst, a local still-life painter, owed Reynier money and may have satisfied that debt by teaching his son. Leonard Bramer is another possibility, although Vermeer's early works seem to reflect nothing of Bramer's style even though their subject matter is similar. There seems to be very little

evidence to support the suggestion that he trained with Gerard ter Borch, high society's favorite genre painter, beyond the fact that they were both witnesses to the same notarial act in a shop in Delft. This may have been nothing more than a coincidental meeting, and there is nothing in Vermeer's youthful works to suggest the influence of Ter Borch, who was fifteen years Vermeer's senior. Ter Borch represented a venerable figural tradition; he studied first in Harleem and then in Amsterdam, and he also made a number of trips throughout Europe. When he came back to the Low Countries, he stopped in Delft and, given the extraordinary ability to observe everyday reality that he employed in making his splendid domestic interiors, he must be included among the possible sources of inspiration for the young Vermeer.

Carel Fabritius is another artist who may have influenced Vermeer's early works. A brilliant pupil of Rembrandt's, Fabritius contributed to the Delft artists' predilection for luminous color tones and an interest in studying and using perspective. Fabritius himself used perspective to expand the boundaries of genre painting, creating such intense spatial constructions that his interior compositions seem full of more profound meaning. He moved Delft in 1650, and two years later he was admitted to the Guild of St. Luke as a master painter. Fabritius's influence was also very important for the next generation of artists in the city. Pieter de Hooch, Emanuel de Witte, and Vermeer himself all borrowed his cool daylight, profound sense of perspective, and the very personal ability to make even very small compositions seem monumental. Some have suggested, based on two sources, that there was a student-teacher relationship between the "Sphinx of Delft" and Rembrandt's pupil. The first is the fact that at the time of his death, Vermeer owned three of Fabritius's pictures, and the second is a debatable interpretation of two verses of a poem by the bookseller and publisher Arnold Bon published in 1668 in Van Bleyswijck's *Description of the City of Delft*. The last quatrain of the poem reads, "Thus did this Phoenix, to our loss, expire / In the midst and at the height of his powers / But happily there arose out of the fire Vermeer, who masterfully trod in his path."

Pieter de Hooch
A Courtyard in Delft
ca. 1660
Mauritshuis,
The Hague

Carel Fabritius was Bon's phoenix; he died in the explosion of Delft's powder magazine in 1654. Some have interpreted the description of Vermeer rising from the phoenix's ashes as a reference to a master-pupil relationship between the two artists. Yet in the final version of the poem, which Bon himself reworked, the last two lines read, "But happily there arose out of the fire Vermeer, who masterfully emulated him." This praise places the younger artist on the same level as Fabritius while not ignoring the difference in their ages. The question has not been completely settled, although other scholars consider it unlikely that Vermeer was Fabritius's pupil. Guild rules stated that an artist could take on pupils only after he had become a master of Delft, a title that came when he was inducted into the Guild of St. Luke. Fabritius obtained that status only fourteen months before Vermeer, and thus the latter would not have had enough time to complete a six-year apprenticeship with the older artist. What is significant about Arnold Bon's poem is that it demonstrates that Vermeer was, by 1668, considered a luminous star in the universe of Dutch painting.

Reynier Jansz Vermeer was buried in the Market Square on October 12, 1652. The fact that no gift was made to the Camer van Charitate, the municipal charity department, at the time of the funeral indicates that the family was impoverished. When his father died Vermeer went back to inn keeping, and shortly afterward, in 1653, his name appears in a document—the first since his baptism—regarding his engagement. The document states that on April 5, 1653, the painter Leonard Bramer and Captain Bartholomeus Melling appeared before a notary at the request of Vermeer and his fiancée, Catharina Bolnes, as witnesses to an agreement made the evening before at the house of Maria Thins, the artist's future mother-in-law. They signed an act of assent to allow the publication of her daughter's marriage banns, as was the custom in the city. Thins had not favored the engagement, although she also agreed not to impede the publication of the banns, thus allowing the notary to sign the certificate in his capacity as a witness. The fact that Bramer witnessed this document has suggested to some scholars that Vermeer must have been studying with him. It is also likely that Maria Thins had initially objected to the marriage on social and religious grounds, and indeed on both points the young Vermeer was hardly an ideal candidate for her daughter's hand. Catharina's mother was a practicing Catholic and belonged to a prominent family from Gouda. Vermeer was a Protestant. And even though he had just recently inherited his father's businesses—the inn and his activity as an art dealer—these were not professions particularly esteemed by the upper economic class. Nonetheless, the wedding was celebrated by a Jesuit priest on Sunday, April 20, 1652, in Schipluy (now known as Schipluiden), a small, Catholic settlement about an hour's walk from Delft. It appears that Vermeer received the Catholic sacraments in that village

Carel Fabritius
The Dismissal of Hagar
1650s
Galleria Sabauda, Turin

church, suggesting he had converted to Catholicism, perhaps at the time of his engagement. All we have, however, are our best guesses. Maria Thins may have made Vermeer's conversion a condition of her tacit consent to his marrying her daughter, and it is likely that the fact that she did not sign the notarial act means that the young Vermeer had not yet converted. Thins offered no objection, however, because she knew that he would do so soon. Vermeer's decision to convert to Catholicism could not have been made lightly, given that Calvinism was essentially the official religion in Holland. It was also an act that both unified the people and gave them something with which to identify. Vermeer seems to have had a good relationship with his mother-in-law. Maria Thins understood painting, and she was a distant relative of the artist Abraham Bloemaert of Utrecht, leading some scholars to suggest that Vermeer thus may have had some contact with him. Catharina's mother also had a modest collection of Utrecht school pictures that she had inherited from her parents, and Vermeer had access to them as soon as he and his wife went to live with her.

Vermeer did in fact reproduce two of these pictures—a *Crucifixion* and *The Procuress*, both by Dirck van Baburen—in his own works.

The young couple, unusual in many ways, lived first at Mechelen, and then in about 1660 they moved to Maria Thins's house in Oude Langendijk, the city's Catholic quarter and home to a Jesuit mission. Vermeer was inscribed as an independent master in the guild on December 29, 1653. He paid only a part of the required fees when he first joined; the rest he paid on July 24, 1656, with funds he borrowed from his mother-in-law. Given the need to supplement the income he earned as a painter to support his growing family, it seems probable that Vermeer continued to run the inn even after he and his wife had moved to her mother's house. Catharina gave birth to fifteen children, four of whom died at a young age. The slow pace at which Vermeer worked meant that he needed to make even more money at other tasks, so in addition to the inn he likely also continued to work in his father's profession as an art dealer. Nonetheless, the artist always preferred to identify himself as "painter" when he signed official documents. He was registered as a painter in the Guild of St. Luke as well, quickly assuming important positions in that organization. Vermeer was appointed twice to a two-year term as dean of the guild, first in 1662 to 1663 and again in 1670 to 1671.

Maria Thins's house must have been large and comfortable, as it accommodated Vermeer's large family. It seems probable, too, that the painter had his studio there and also used that space for his work as an art dealer. We can guess at what his studio looked like from the numerous pictures in which he painted easels, a heavy oak table, and leather-upholstered chairs with carved arms.

Scholars do not agree on the identification of Vermeer's earliest works. There is, in particular, a group of paintings some experts attribute to the youthful artist while others exclude them, noting important differences, both in style and technique, with his later works. The fact that none of these pictures is documented and the signatures in each is different—in some cases it may even have been added later—has reinforced the doubts. We know, furthermore, that there was a contemporary of Vermeer's active in Delft who was known, among other names, as Jan van der Meer of Utrecht, and some of the works in question here have occasionally been assigned to him. The subject matter of these early works, datable to about 1655, fuels the debate over their attribution, although it is not improbable that Vermeer would have tested himself at the beginning of his career with religious and mythological subjects. These works would have been called history paintings in the seventeenth century; in his *Schilderboeck* ("Book of Painters"), Karel van Mander identified "history painting" as the most important artistic genre. Yet the choice of subject matter does apparently separate these works from the rest of Vermeer's oeuvre, which is characterized

by scenes of everyday life. Still other scholars insist that these pictures must be considered the fruit of Vermeer's slow production.

This group of paintings includes a *Saint Praxedis* (Barbara Piasecka Johnson Collection Foundation, Princeton, N.J.), which can be dated from between 1653 and 1655. Although the truth of these attributions may never be known, Vermeer may have executed these few history paintings with large figures to demonstrate his abilities to the guild. For those who believe that the *Saint Praxedis* is an autograph work by Vermeer, the picture, a copy of another by the Florentine Felice Ficherelli (ca. 1645, Fergnani Collection, Ferrara, Italy), is closely associated with the artist's conversion to Catholicism in 1653. In this sense the religious subject would affirm Vermeer's commitment to his new faith. The date of the work (1655) and two signatures discovered on the canvas, the second of which has been deciphered as "(Ver)Meer N(aar) R(ip)o(s)o"—that is, "Vermeer from an original by Riposo" (Ficherelli's nickname)—offer some evidence that the attribution is correct. A comparison of the Italian original with the copy reveals that the technique used to paint the sky in the background is similar in both. That process was fairly unusual among Dutch painters, consisting of layering ultramarine over a darker color to achieve the desired effect. Vermeer chose, however, to render the saint's face in a more intimate and delicate manner, softening her features by outlining them with short brushstrokes. Saint Praxedis' face and her reflective attitude—indicated by her lowered eyes—recall the women Vermeer painted in his later works. The most important difference from the Italian original, however, is the crucifix Vermeer placed in the saint's hand, underscoring the artist's religious feelings. It also suggests the symbolic union of Christ's blood with that of the Christian martyrs, which Praxedis has soaked up with a sponge to be preserved in a reliquary. This and similar observations suggest to those who believe Vermeer painted the *Saint Praxedis* that it was made for personal reasons or perhaps for someone in Maria Thins's circle, which was closely allied with the Jesuits. One might also ask how and when Vermeer could have seen Ficherelli's work. There are, however, no documents that put Vermeer in Delft between 1650 and 1653, so it is possible that he traveled to Italy, perhaps at the suggestion of Leonard Bramer, who had

Attributed to
Johannes Vermeer
Saint Praxedis
40 x 32 1/2 inches
(101.6 x 82.6 cm)
Barbara Piasecka Johnson
Collection Foundation,
Prineton, N.J.

made a similar study trip himself. Vermeer's relationship to Italian art is a tricky question. We can be sure that he knew and appreciated the work of the Utrecht *Caravaggisti*, the Dutch followers of Caravaggio, which he saw in his mother-in-law's collection. An event in 1672, however, suggests that Vermeer had a more profound knowledge of Italian painting. He and Jacob Jordaens were summoned to The Hague to judge the authenticity of a group of Italian pictures that the Elector of Brandenburg had purchased for an exorbitant price from a dealer in Amsterdam. Both painters declared in front of a notary that these paintings were "garbage and without the least value." There were certainly Italian pictures to be seen in Amsterdam and Utrecht in that period—and copies of them in Delft—but it is also true that in the seventeenth century Italian painting was not always considered superior to that of the Low Countries. This was the result of a new, middle-class interest in art, and it was strong enough that Vermeer himself chose self-consciously to explore his own artistic heritage, demonstrating an awareness of Jan van Eyck's analytical use of light.

In addition to the *Saint Praxedis*, two other paintings have provoked debate and a variety of opinions. They are the *Christ in the House of Martha and Mary* (National Gallery of Scotland, Edinburgh) and *Diana and Her Nymphs* (Mauritshuis, The Hague), both of which can be dated to about 1655 or 1656. Those who attribute all three to Vermeer point to the similar technique of layering different colors to achieve a greater sense of luminosity in the draperies. The *Christ in the House of Martha and Mary*, the result it seems of a specific commission, demonstrates Vermeer's independence from traditional painting in Delft. It is closer to the Utrecht school and especially to the works of Abraham Bloemaert (the distant relative of Maria Thins) and Hendrick ter Brugghen, although it is most similar to the large painting of the same subject by the Flemish artist, Erasmus Quellinus II (*Christ in the House of Martha and Mary*, ca. 1645, Musée des Beaux-Arts, Valenciennes). Here, too, a hypothetical study trip would have allowed the artist to see these precedents. If we accept that the work is by Vermeer, then his sophisticated theological interpretation of the Gospel account is interesting. While Quellinus suggests that the contemplative life (represented by Mary, who sits listening at Christ's feet) is preferable to the active one (personified by Martha, who is intent on serving food), Vermeer seems to want to say that the union of the two is the true and only path to salvation. An analysis of the three figures offers a similar conclusion; in Vermeer's painting they are all contained almost entirely within a triangular block, while in Quellinus's Martha is on one side and Mary and Christ are on the other. Thus Vermeer touched on one of the fundamental points in the theological dispute between Protestants and Catholics, who disagreed about whether grace was bestowed by God alone (the former) or could be earned through faith and good

Opposite, with details on the following pages:
Attributed to Johannes Vermeer
Christ in the House of Martha and Mary
1655–1656, oil on canvas
5.2 x 4.6 ft. (160 x 141 cm)
National Gallery of Scotland, Edinburgh

works (the latter). Presuming the scene is originally meant as a celebration of the contemplative life over the active one, this picture might also suggest a provocative parallel between the Gospel story and Vermeer's own life. Like Mary, the artist from a very early age had preferred intellectual pursuits to the more frenetic activities at the inn. The signature on the canvas reads "IVMeer." It has been taken as evidence that the work is by "Vermeer of Delft," while those who reject the attribution see it as pointing to the authorship of "Johan van der Meer of Utrecht." Other experts believe the signature is a fake, and they reject the attribution to Vermeer on the basis of the expressiveness of the painting as well as its technique and stylistic characteristics.

In *Diana and Her Nymphs*, the theme of care and attention "toward someone" turns from the religious to the mythological, because it is now a classical goddess who is the center of attention. The painting includes a barely legible monogram ("VM"). We can also compare it with Jacob van Loo's *Diana and Her Nymphs*, dated about 1650 (Herzog Anton Ulrich Museum, Brunswick). Vermeer's painting has a silence and solemnity as well as a dominant immobility that will become a characteristic of all of his later works. This effect is achieved in part by hiding or shading the figures' eyes, to suggest a sense of calm. Vermeer may have learned this device, so masterfully developed by Rembrandt, from his contacts with Fabritius. The same is not true in Van Loo's work, in which a play of glances animates the figures and suggests a dynamism and tension. Vermeer's warmer colors, perhaps influenced by Italian painting, also create an elegiac and dreamlike atmosphere. There is also what Jean Cocteau defined as a *côté insolite*, an ensemble of incongruous elements that the painter used to create an aura of mystery in the composition—the nymph who turns her back on the principal action, the plate and towel in the foreground, the thistle

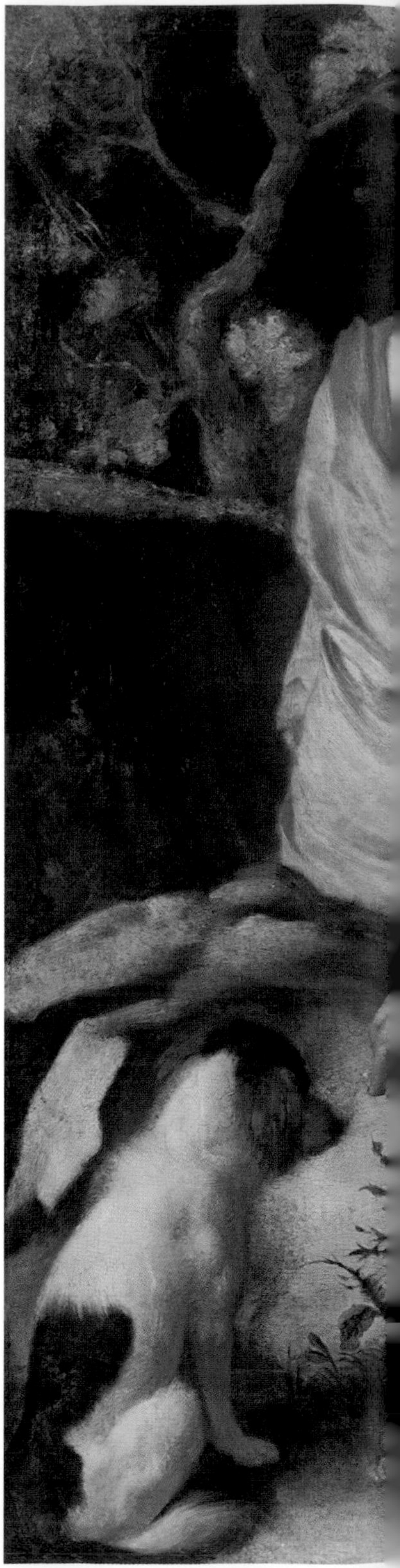

Attributed to
Johannes Vermeer
Diana and Her Nymphs
ca. 1655–1656, oil on canvas
3.2 x 3.4 ft. (98.5 x 105 cm)
Mauritshuis,
The Hague

plant between Diana and the rock to suggest the imminent arrival of Acteon, who is, however, physically absent from the representation.

The similarities in color between this group of three paintings and *The Procuress* (Staatliche Kunstsammlungen, Gemäldegalerie, Dresden), dated 1656 and also much debated, is considered a strong argument in sustaining the attributions of the earlier works to Vermeer. If it is an autograph work, *The Procuress* would represent Vermeer's passage from subjects appropriate to history painting to genre scenes. The great originality of the artist's work is first fully expressed in 1656 when he abandons religious and mythological subjects and turns instead to the reality of his own time. Bearing in mind that some scholars have disputed this attribution, *The Procuress* certainly draws some inspiration from Dirck van Baburen's painting of the same subject (*The Procuress*, 1622, Museum of Fine Arts, Boston), which Maria Thins owned at the time her son-in-law and his family came to live with her. She had obtained it as part of the settlement that followed her separation from her husband, in 1641, and we can be sure that Vermeer knew of the picture because he borrowed from it for two of his own paintings—*The Concert* (Isabella Stewart Gardner Museum, formerly Boston, stolen in 1990) of 1664 to 1666 and *A Young Woman Seated at a Virginal* (National Gallery, London) of 1672 to 1673. The size of *The Procuress* and its large figures also connect it to the group of early works; otherwise, it opened a new chapter in Vermeer's career as he turned to simple representations of scenes from everyday life that offered moral lessons. *The Procuress* touches on the subject of the commerce of love as facilitated by wine in order to admonish as well as offer a norm for good behavior. It is possible that the association of secular subjects with lessons in morality was tied to the new phenomenon of a middle class, influenced by the moral rigor of the Reformation, engaged in collecting art. Furthermore, in *The Procuress*, unlike the earlier paintings, Vermeer introduces a sense of action—

Right, with details on the following pages:
Attributed to
Johannes Vermeer
The Procuress
1656, oil on canvas
4.7 x 4.3 ft. (143 x 130 cm)
Staatliche Kunstsammlungen,
Gemäldegalerie,
Dresden

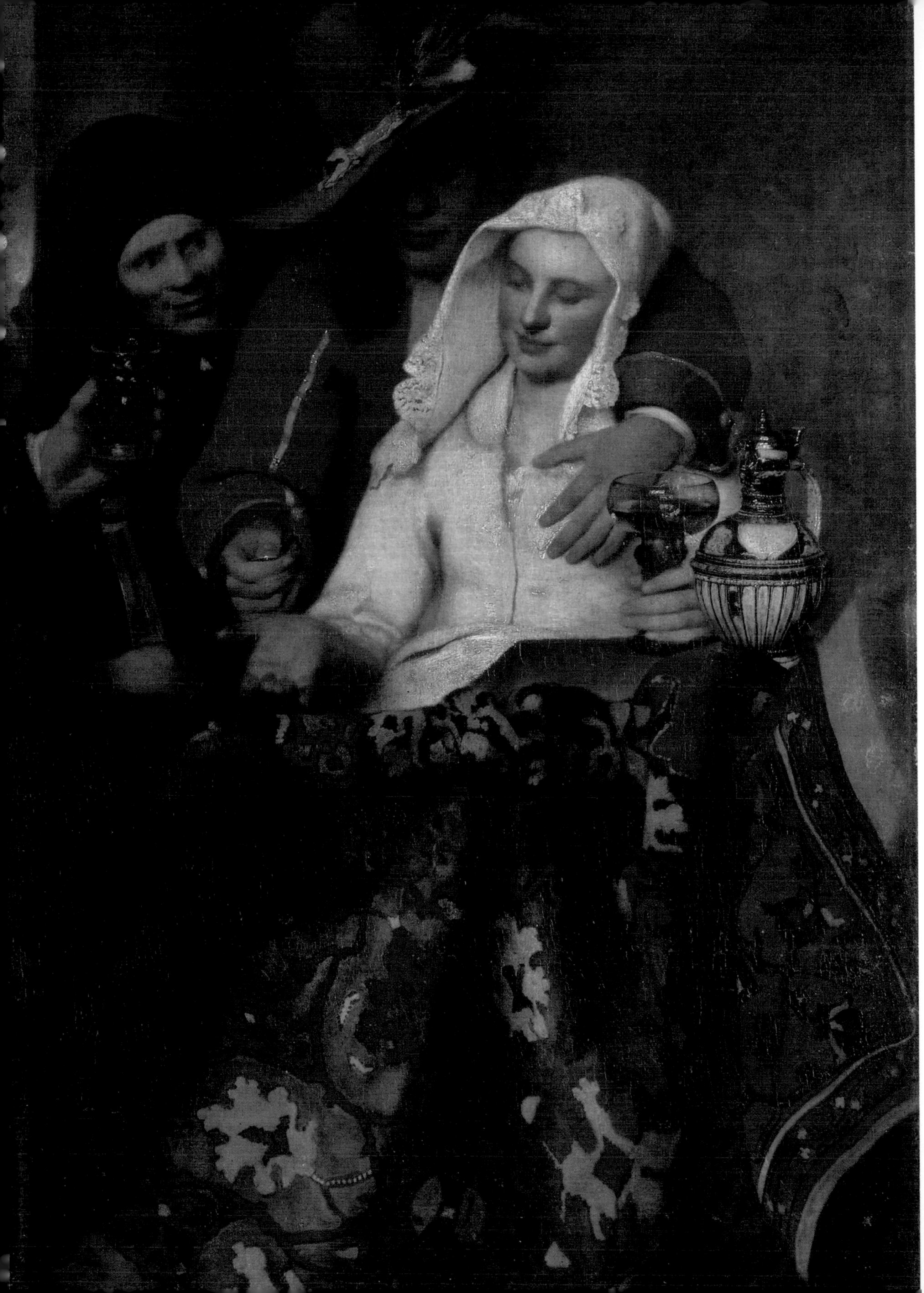

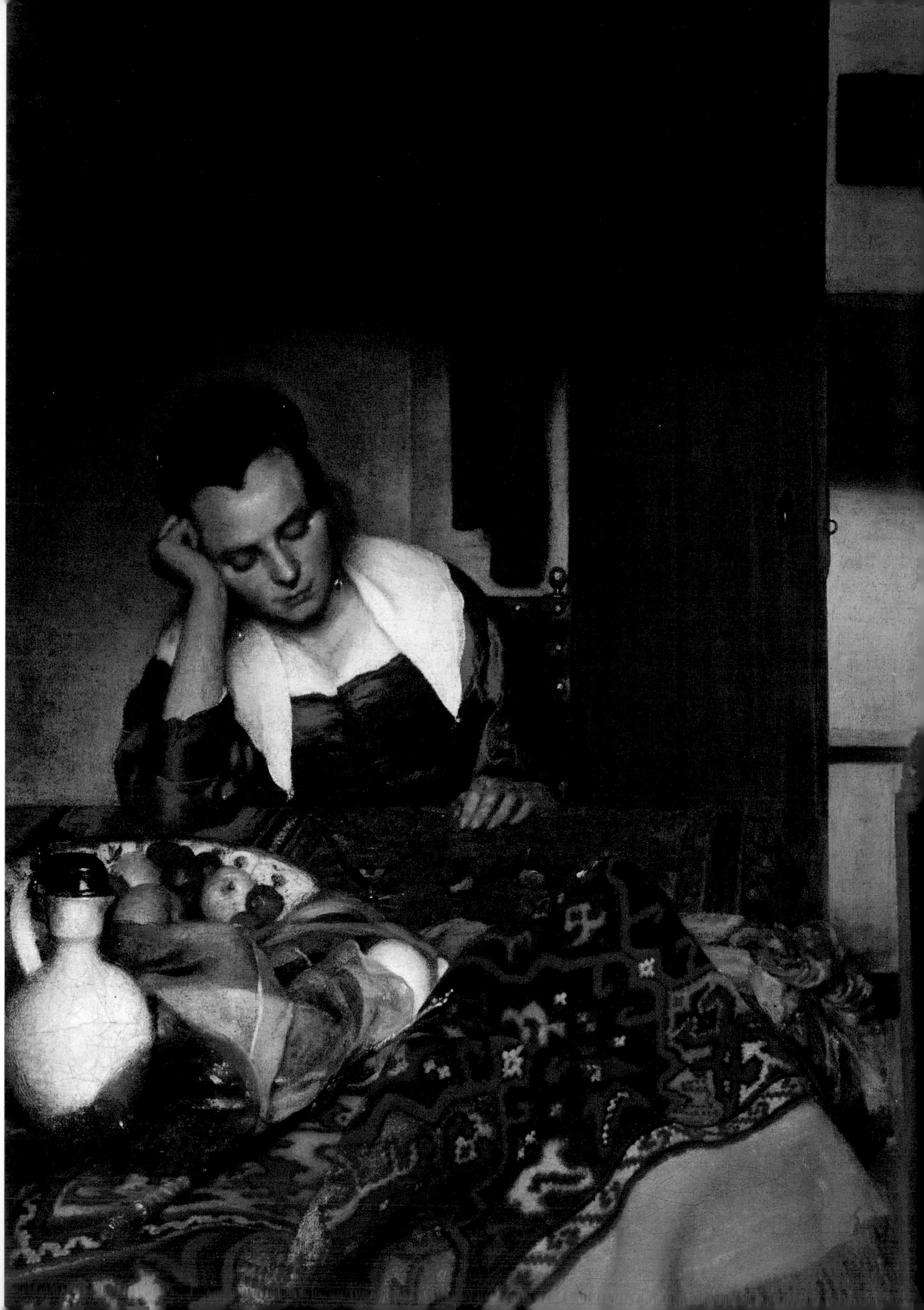

in the play of hands, the angle of the suitor's hat, and the slight inclination of the woman's head; the works that follow it will recover the sense of silence and immobility that are the hallmarks of this painter's style.

The Maid Asleep (The Metropolitan Museum of Art, New York) is thought to date from only a little later than *The Procuress*, about 1657, and the two works have similarities in both style and composition—for example in the intense red and yellow highlights and the richly decorated carpets in the foregrounds. In the painting at the Metropolitan Museum, the artist is clearly interested in creating a more convincing space for his subject, which is also where the viewer's gaze immediately is drawn. The maid is framed by a square formed by the edge of the table, the doorjamb, and the frame of the picture hanging above the woman; the viewer is led to her by the oblique placement of the chair. The inventory of the auction held in Amsterdam on May 16, 1696, lists this picture as *A Drunken Girl Sleeping at a Table*, making the semantically open character of the work clear. Leaning her head on her hand, a jug of wine in the foreground, the fruit dish, the man in the next room who was later painted out, and the dark painting above the woman with a *putto* or a cupid and a mask are all symbolic elements perfectly orchestrated to transmit a moralizing message. Sloth and the drowsiness caused by too much wine are condemned here, the latter especially leading to neglecting responsibilities and giving in to vice. The allusion to an extramarital relationship and its risks were abandoned here, but they return in other works by Vermeer. The strength of his paintings lies in the possibility of different readings because every element in the compositions remains open from a semantic point of view. Beginning with *The Maid Asleep*, the artist introduces the viewer with great delicacy to a feminine universe, unveiling an intimacy that can be seen only in well-hidden and private places.

Left, with details on
the following pages:
Johannes Vermeer
The Maid Asleep
ca. 1657, oil on canvas
2.9 x 2.5 ft. (87.5 x 76.5 cm)
The Metropolitan
Museum of Art,
New York

There is another picture from this period that focuses on drinking. It is the *Officer and Laughing Girl* (1656–1657, Frick Collection, New York), and here Vermeer portrays the unfolding process of seduction assisted, again, by drunkenness. The officer dominates the scene even though he is turned around and almost completely in shadow. The light coming in through the side window illuminates the man as well as the map hanging on the wall and the girl, who is transformed into a symphony of luminosity. These are the elements, furthermore, that became the recurring motifs in Vermeer's pictures, their deeper meaning denying the apparent monotony of the compositions. The military officer in the painting may reflect Vermeer's familiarity with and interest in soldiers. He enrolled in the civic militia of Delft in 1664, perhaps because of the threat of war with England, which broke out in the following year. Service in a civilian militia, especially in times of peace, was a way for a good citizen to fulfill his duty to the community. When soldiers appear in Vermeer's works, however, the noise that normally accompanies group portraits of members of civic militias gives way instead to a sense of silence and intimacy.

The decisive shift in Vermeer's technique, particularly in his handling of light, is visible in *Officer and Laughing Girl*, but then even more so in the *Girl Reading a Letter at an Open Window* (Staatliche Kunstsammlungen, Gemäldegalerie, Dresden) of 1657. Before these two pictures, Vermeer seemed almost to ignore the interest most painters of the Delft school (including Paulus Potter, Geraerd Houckgeest, and Carel Fabritius) had in light. Beginning with them, however, he concentrated primarily on the effects of light, finally arriving at the point of drawing with colors and modeling forms with light.

Right, with details on the following pages:
Johannes Vermeer
Officer and Laughing Girl
ca. 1656–1657, oil on canvas
1.6 x 1.4 ft. (48 x 43 cm)
The Frick Collection,
New York

NOVA ET ACCVRATA TOTIVS HOLLANDIÆ WESTFRISIÆQ TOPOGRAPHIA

HOLLANDIÆ WESTFRISIÆQ TOPOGRAPHIA

Opposite, with details
on the following pages:
Johannes Vermeer
Girl Reading a Letter at an Open Window
1657, oil on canvas
2.7 x 2.1 ft. (83 x 64.5 cm)
Staatliche Kunstsammlungen,
Gemäldegalerie,
Dresden

GIRL READING A LETTER AT AN OPEN WINDOW

In *Officer and Laughing Girl*, Vermeer borrows something of Pieter de Hooch's boldly constructed interior spaces; a little later he simplifies that scheme in his *Girl Reading a Letter at an Open Window*, painted in 1657 and now in Dresden. One of the artist's most extraordinary abilities was in using the repertoire of contemporary genre painting and then sublimating the devices by the extreme simplification of their compositional elements. This takes him beyond the simple observation of everyday events.

In this painting, Vermeer has stripped away almost every narrative element that animated the works of De Hooch, concentrating instead on a solitary figure, engrossed and silent and surrounded by inanimate objects. The wall, a window, a curtain, and a fruit dish on a carpet-covered table are the immobile objects that frame the image of intense concentration—a young woman completely detached from the world around her. This is the salient characteristic of Vermeer's aesthetic and of his originality, which can express so much without saying a lot.

Unlike De Hooch, Vermeer does not flood his interior with light, which would disrupt the reflective atmosphere enveloping the young woman, who appears to be the protagonist of "a secret scene, secretly observed." The subject of the painting is the letter, a love letter, as we now know from the X-ray that revealed that Vermeer had originally included a cupid in the composition as a sort of key to reading the scene. The window is open, illuminating an otherwise nearly completely darkened room. The open window also functions to underscore the woman's hidden desire to reveal her space to the outside world, a space that the rigid rules of social behavior devised as a means of isolating her from that world. The fruit dish on the table could, in this sense, symbolize the extramarital relationship in which this young woman is likely involved.

In this canvas, as in the earlier *Officer and Laughing Girl*, the painter uses his famous pointillism, a particular pictorial technique in which he dabbed small dots of white paint on the areas that were meant to be the most brightly lit. They appear in the still life in the foreground, the folds of the woman's jacket, and in her hair; these patches of light are droplets of pure color accompanied by their subtle iridescence. Some scholars believe that Vermeer obtained this effect—"more real than reality"—by using optical instruments such as a double concave lens mounted in a camera obscura. We can also conclude, inevitably, that he was influenced by Rembrandt, who was also very concerned with creating his desired effects by highlighting color against deeper tones.

Chapter 2
Painter of Light

Vermeer had finished his training by the end of the 1650s, having absorbed from other artists—including Van Baburen, Van Loo, Fabritius, Nicolaes Maes, and Pieter de Hooch—what he wanted for his own style. This did not happen quickly, and Vermeer was behind his contemporaries in assimilating discoveries about the handling of light and space. Whether because of his slow formation or not, Vermeer entered his mature period as a skilled master, the ground well prepared for his future masterpieces.

In the years before Vermeer moved in with his mother-in-law, the number of artists in Delft fell; many of them moved away and most to Amsterdam. This meant that the deans of the Guild of St. Luke, usually older artists, were now nominated from among such younger members as Vermeer. He was chosen for the position more to fill a void than for his own precociousness. The art scene in Delft remained as lively as before, and the city continued to be an important transit center and place where artists met, as they had easy access to the various art collections in the city.

In the period between 1657 and 1658, Vermeer abandoned biblical and mythological subject matter (assuming that the youthful works attributed to him are autograph compositions) and concentrated entirely on genre scenes and landscapes. Once again why the "Sphinx of Delft" changed course is not known, although this time we do have some clues that allow us to reconstruct this moment in his career. They come in the form of two artists, Pieter de Hooch and Jan Steen, who came to Delft in 1654 and 1655, respectively. Their works offered Vermeer useful examples of the fusing of everyday figurative and architectural elements to give life to a new vision of reality. Each painter did this in his own way, and their relationships with Vermeer need to be seen as mutual exchanges of stimuli and suggestions. Over time Vermeer came to surpass these inspirations with his extraordinary sense of composition. Steen was well known for his innovative genre scenes, and he had earned his reputation before he came to Delft, where he rented a pub to supplement his income. His paintings are a sort of bantering counterpoint to Vermeer's pictures, which are immersed in an absolute silence. De Hooch, however, began to explore his interest in space and

Johannes Vermeer
Young Woman with a Water Pitcher (detail)
1662–1665, oil on canvas
1.5 x 1.3 ft. (45.7 x 40.5 cm)
The Metropolitan Museum of Art, New York

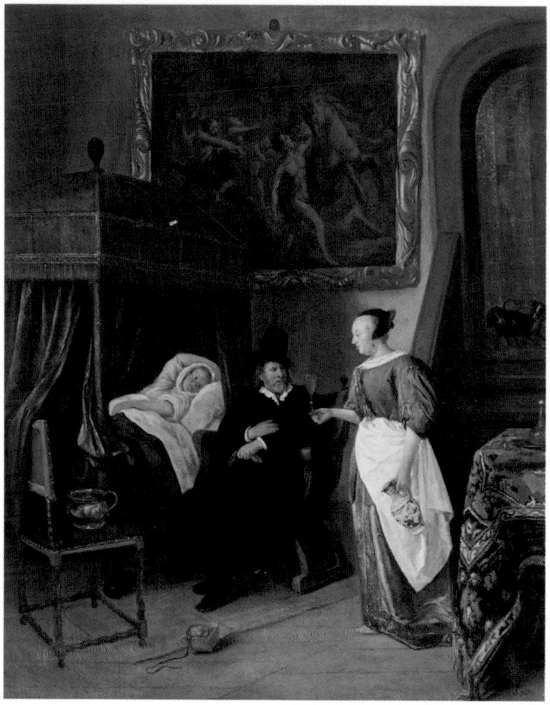

architectural compositions only shortly after he had enrolled in the guild. His pictures represent middle-class interiors and courtyards in which light has a decisive role in defining the relationship between his figures. De Hooch became a delicate interpreter of calmness; quiet dominates his domestic interiors—he was a kind of alter ego to Vermeer, but without his poetic gifts. Even though any relationship between Vermeer and De Hooch is undocumented, it is very likely that they knew each other, given what their works have in common. We can imagine Vermeer was aware, from the beginning, of how his slightly older colleague handled light, but it was also doubtless the case that at a certain point their roles were reversed, creating a reciprocal exchange. Both offered views into intimate interiors, but with differences in their approaches to representing them. De Hooch carefully described external details, while Vermeer explored the psychological meaning hidden behind the surface of each small object.

Vermeer's continuing economic problems most likely explains why he entered into an exclusive relationship with Pieter Claesz van Ruijven, a well-to-do, middle-class collector. Some scholars have also suggested that the artist's shift from historical to genre subjects was the result of an agreement between the two men and linked to a loan Van Ruijven made to Vermeer in 1657. Not all experts

Left:
Jan Steen
The Tooth Puller
1651
Mauritshuis,
The Hague

Right:
Jan Steen
The Doctor's Visit
1650s
Mauritshuis,
The Hague

agree, however, that Vermeer used his pictures as an alternate form of payment. Van Ruijven owned twenty-one of Vermeer's paintings; they were eventually offered for sale in Amsterdam in 1696. Given, too, that the collector left the painter 500 florins in the will Van Ruijven's widow drew up in 1665, it seems that the relationship between the two families was a strong one.

Left:
Pieter de Hooch
Woman Drinking with Soldiers
1658
Louvre Museum, Paris

Right:
Pieter de Hooch
The Mistress and Her Maid
After 1663
Hermitage Museum, St. Petersburg

What about Johannes and Catharina's life together once they moved to the Catholic quarter? After he converted, Vermeer was part of a religious minority in a city dominated by Protestants, although his membership in the civic militia suggests that he continued to have relationships with at least some part of the Protestant community. In those years Protestants were still repressing Catholicism; in Delft the most substantial presence of the Catholic Church was that of the Jesuit community in the area around "Papist Corner." We have no information regarding the contact Vermeer may have had with his own family after his marriage. The painter did not attend the christening of his niece, his sister Gertruy's daughter, and the fact that he named none of his fifteen children after either his mother or his father, as was then the custom, suggests that he wanted to keep a certain distance from his own past. At the same time Vermeer insisted that his parents' portraits hang in the main living room of his mother-in-law's house, indicating that he did not completely deny his family origins. On February 1, 1661, Maria Thins visited her sick sister, Cornelia, and on that occasion Cornelia called a notary to ratify and approve Catharina's marriage to Vermeer. After Cornelia died, Catharina inherited a considerable income, more than Vermeer himself earned from his painting and art dealing together. It was not enough, however, to maintain their family for a lifetime. The slow rhythm with which Vermeer produced his paintings did not allow him economic security, and he was often dependent on regular loans or monetary support from his mother-in-law. Vermeer's sluggish production is evidenced by a visit he had from a French diplomat and art connoisseur. In August 1663, Balthasar de Monconys spent several days in Delft. After leaving for a little more than a week, he returned with the express purpose of meeting with Vermeer, but Monconys noted in his diary that he was not able to see any of his pictures because the artist had no inventory in his studio. His only opportunity to see a work by Vermeer came from a baker who owned one of his paintings. Hendrick van Buyten, the baker and a man who would be very important in settling the artist's estate, showed Monconys and his companions the painting he had bought from Vermeer; by the time Van Buyten died, in 1701, he owned three of them. The French diplomat's opinion, moreover, was that Van Buyten had paid too much for a picture with only one figure. This episode handily demonstrates how different Vermeer's working method was from that of many of his contemporaries, who always had enough of their own work to exhibit on their walls. It also confirms that the two or three works Vermeer produced a year were tied to specific commissions. Initially, however, his pictures did not command especially high prices, and it was only after the 1696 auction that this began to change. Living in Maria Thins's house allowed the important advantage of saving on rent, and it also offered the artist the possibility of making contacts that could lead to new commissions. Furthermore, it explains why Vermeer, unlike so many of his contemporaries, never left Delft for another city with a more active art scene.

Vermeer's pictures from the late 1550s allow us to speculate, based on the visual evidence of his painted interiors, a little about his family life. Every interior scene that took shape on his canvases was the result of a careful and meticulous choice of objects introduced as "co-protagonists" in each of his compositions. Nothing was left to chance. We can imagine that Vermeer sometimes constructed "sets" in the room in Maria Thins's big house that served as his studio, carefully studying how he might arrange on the canvas the objects he had in front of him. There is nothing obvious in his scenes; he simply patiently described an everyday existence. The objects he chose were never placed randomly, because their position, proportions, color, and surface qualities always interacted harmoniously with the figures. Although he did not specialize

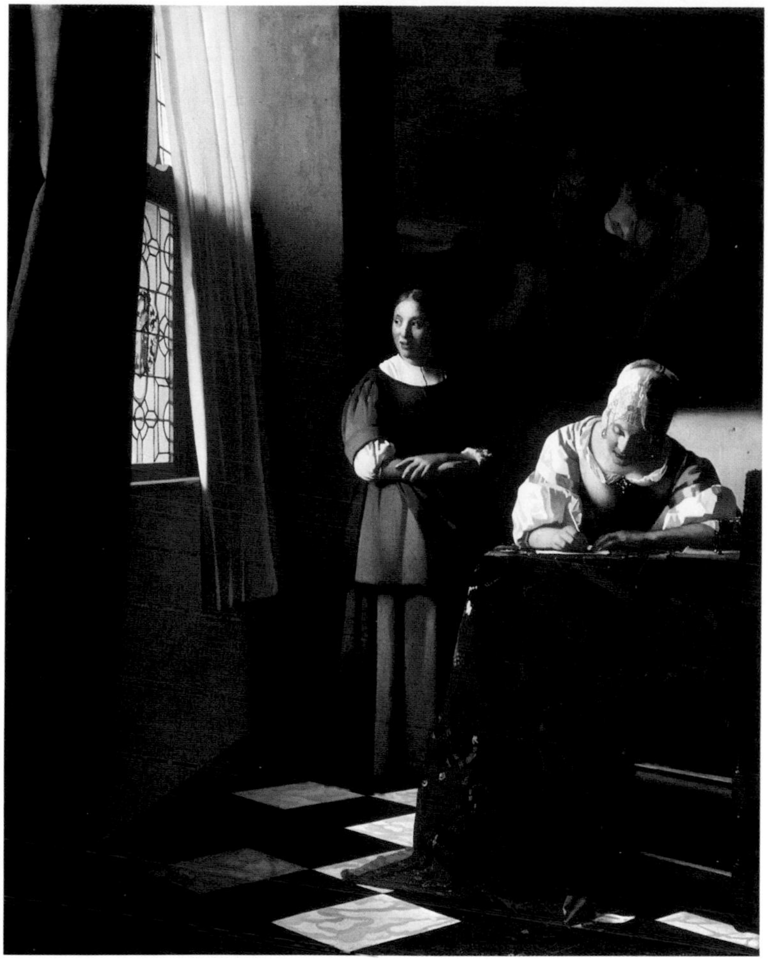

Johannes Vermeer
Lady Writing a Letter with Her Maid
ca. 1670, oil on canvas
2.3 x 2 ft. (71.1 x 60.5 cm)
National Gallery of Ireland, Dublin

exclusively in interior scenes, Vermeer was nonetheless unique in his extraordinary capacity to create reflections of situations and types that not only defined a specific period or culture, but were also examples of a universal human psychology. In general his works contain important admonitions about the nature of existence, offering some sort of moral guidance for human behavior. To accomplish this Vermeer stripped his compositions of everything useless or superfluous. In reducing his "intimate" stories to a minimum number of allusions, the artist came very close to Rembrandt, who, in a similar way, cleared his visual imagination of even the smallest details that he considered banal or unnecessary. Rembrandt was born in Leyden in 1609, and he may have exercised some influence on the young Vermeer's handling of light and color through his students in Delft (Leonard Bramer and Carel Fabritius). That influence seems to be reflected in the works Vermeer made in the middle years of his career; their more refined and contained brushstrokes were perhaps necessary because the subjects and messages he painted required an almost crystalline clarity. After painting *The Procuress* of 1656, Vermeer gradually moved toward images that

were more self-absorbed and removed from the noisy outside world. It is almost as if the artist discovered a new beauty hidden in common things, which required, in turn, that he represent them absolutely faithfully. Vermeer's work of this period seems almost revolutionary, challenging the myth that action should be the main actor in a painting. In these pictures the figure is the true object of the viewer's gaze, and it has been passed through a series of sentimental and intellectual filters. Vermeer's scenes were, thanks to the choices he made with regard to reality, true and eternal portraits of the middle-class life in his bourgeois city. At the same time they were packed with symbolism and allegories that helped maintain a sense of the people's identity. The pictures' apparent meanings are revealed in the reality they represent—charged with important significance for the life of the times. And while the paintings might seem empty of any content or filled only with decorative elements, they point instead to a universe of connotation.

The *Girl with a Wine Glass* (Herzog Anton Ulrich-Museum, Brunswick, Germany) is one of Vermeer's first interior scenes as well as a precocious

Rembrandt van Rijn
Parable of the Laborers in the Vineyard
1637
Hermitage Museum,
St. Petersburg

Opposite:
Johannes Vermeer
Girl with a Wine Glass
ca. 1658–1660, oil on canvas
2.6 x 2.2 ft. (78 x 67.5 cm)
Herzog Anton Ulrich-Museum,
Brunswick

example of the artist's ability to paint subtle psychological representations. It can be dated from between 1658 and 1660, and depicts a seduction unfolding in a bourgeois interior. If we compare this picture with the slightly earlier *Officer and Laughing Woman* (Frick Collection, New York), Vermeer here creates a greater distance between the figures and the viewer, toward whom the young woman turns her gaze. Her smile seems to say that she is accepting both the glass of wine and the amorous attentions of one of the men present in the room. The moralizing undercurrent in the scene emerges in the objects placed around the figures. The painting hanging on the back wall of the room is a portrait of the woman's husband, who remains watchful although he is physically absent, and the man in the background perhaps plays the role of go-between for the suitor. The stained-glass quatrefoil decoration in the partially opened window also carries a moralizing message. It includes a coat-of-arms, and above it, a personification of Temperance taken from the book of emblems that Gabriel Rollenhagen published in 1611. This allegorical figure is accompanied by her attributes, including a square (to act with justice) and a bridle (to rein in emotions).

A window with the same motif appears in another of Vermeer's works—*The Glass of Wine* (Staatliche Museen, Gemäldegalerie, Berlin)—that was painted at more or less the same time. The figure of Temperance is here placed directly in the woman's

Johannes Vermeer
Girl with a Wine Glass (detail)
ca. 1658–1660, oil on canvas
2.6 x 2.2 ft. (78 x 67.5 cm)
Herzog Anton Ulrich-Museum, Brunswick

line of vision as a sort of admonishment. The *Girl with a Wine Glass*, which depicts a man who has just given a woman a glass of wine to weaken her resistance to his advances, returns to the themes of human weakness and the danger of excess. Both pictures fit into the general category of domestic scenes—often commenting on themes of love and courtship—common in Holland in the middle of the seventeenth century. Vermeer's representations are unique, though, because he created interiors in which the action seems frozen in a moment of reflection. His technique also noticeably improved in these two works; he focuses on a delicacy of execution well suited to the tastes and expectations of sophisticated patrons. A short time later Vermeer would again demonstrate how skillfully he was able to adapt his technique to a particular subject. One need only think of *The Kitchen Maid* (Rijksmuseum, Amsterdam) of 1658 to 1660, in which the humble figure of the woman is defined by vigorous, painterly brushstrokes.

Many of Vermeer's works from this period are characterized by a single female figure in a domestic interior captured at a moment that seems almost to freeze her movement specifically in order to express some spiritual or allusive meaning. The female universe was full of profound significance for Vermeer, particularly because women had a special role in Dutch society. It was a woman's duty to keep the house in order and to look after her family, even if betrayal lurked behind the appearance of respectable middle-class values. Vermeer entered this complicated, female universe very cautiously. He was able to catch a barely uttered sigh, a stifled smile, or a fleeting facial expression and transfer it to his canvases where silence was almost absolute, broken only briefly and almost inaudibly by the slightest of sounds. The women in his paintings are figures without names or histories, yet Vermeer condenses in each a restrained modesty and joy—or perhaps some agitation and emotion—and he uses them then to communicate profound meaning.

The everyday world around Vermeer furnished the artist both with inspiration for his subject matter and the very objects he would use to "construct" the settings for each of his works. And although the room Vermeer represents seems always to be the same, its space is continuously transformed into something new according

Right, with details on the following pages:
The Glass of Wine
ca. 1658–1660, oil on canvas
2.2 x 2.5 ft. (66.3 x 76.5 cm)
Staatliche Museen, Gemäldegalerie, Berlin

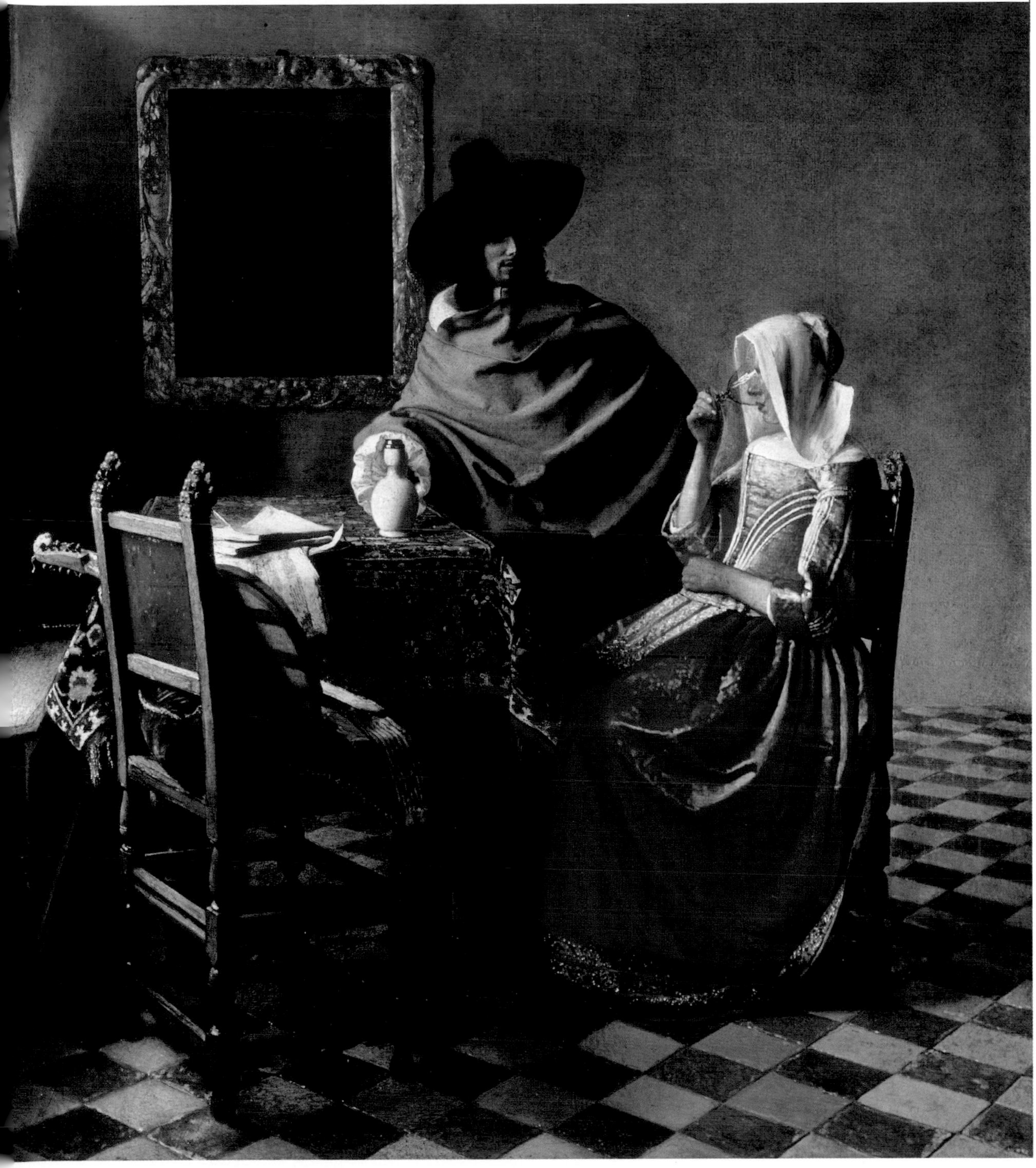

Opposite, with details
on the following pages:
Johannes Vermeer
The Kitchen Maid
1658–1660, oil on canvas
1.5 x 1.3 ft. (45.5 x 41 cm)
Rijksmuseum,
Amsterdam

THE KITCHEN MAID

Now in the Rijksmuseum in Amsterdam, Vermeer's *The Kitchen Maid* is one of his most famous works, considered second only to the *View of Delft* and much appreciated shortly after the artist's death. It was sold at auction in 1696 for the extraordinary sum of 175 florins.

This picture is generally associated with the small group of paintings in Vermeer's oeuvre identified as *exempla virtuti*—intended to offer positive examples of good conduct. The others are the *Young Woman with a Water Pitcher* and *The Lace Maker*. The artist from Delft painted this small work between 1658 and 1660, at a time when his interest in everyday scenes and the beauty hidden behind the ordinary appearance of things first flowered; this theme would remain the focus of his work for the rest of his life. *The Kitchen Maid* recalls a genre of similar scenes that already existed in the Low Countries. In his version of the type, however, Vermeer abandoned any references that might be read as a criticism of serving women. The maid is the only figure in the scene, and she appears to be neither distracted nor lazy and concentrates instead on her work. Her eyes are lowered, a sign of humility and modest meditation, and she is pouring milk from a pitcher into a terracotta bowl with extreme care. All her attention is focused on not spilling a drop of the milk, an aspect that has suggested to a number of scholars that she is a symbolic image of Temperance, a virtue the Dutch held especially dear at the time. In reality the fact that she stands in the corner of a simple and undecorated room communicates a powerful moral and physical presence in and of itself.

In this work Vermeer had demonstrated a real mastery in blending technique and content, using a vigorous, robust brushstroke well suited to the woman's physical energy. This energy derives from her strong physique and is extolled by the moral value of the work she does—it provides necessary sustenance, a notion underscored by the loaf of bread in the basket in the foreground. The simple still life on the kitchen table, moreover, offers yet another example of Vermeer's dizzying ability to represent real objects; here he does not disdain to represent each small detail of the simple objects with minute care.

The link between figures and space is carefully studied in all of Vermeer's interior scenes; in this case it is the element that characterizes the entire composition. The servant's robust character and her rustic features are in perfect harmony with the simple room in which there are few things—a pail and basket hanging on the wall and the brazier on the floor—to distract attention from the principal figure. The artist achieved his effect through perspective and light, manipulated in such a way that they visually reinforce the value of what the maid is doing. The meeting of the orthogonal lines that construct the space, and especially its raking illumination, in concert define the "soul" of the scene, personified in the monumental, vigorous form of the woman. As he worked on the scene Vermeer chose to eliminate anything that might distract attention from the main theme of the painting, modifying the wall behind the maid that at first had something—perhaps a map—hanging on it.

The Kitchen Maid quickly became a symbol of Holland itself, as much for its subject and her dignity as for its fame. It is significant that Vermeer used here a compositional format typical of history paintings (as, for example, in the *Queen Artemisia* of about 1645 by a follower of Domenico Fiasella) as the basis for his scene of everyday life. In this way his image acquired a lasting significance: the maid stands there, real and tangible, but at the same time she transcends time and place. Her presence has something eternal about it, as if she will never stop so carefully pouring her milk.

to the person who was to inhabit it. The painter's images distilled the visual impressions he took from the physical world, exposing the internal harmony of ordinary life—especially within the walls of a home.

Most of Vermeer's paintings feature women as their protagonists and belong in the general category of admonition against vice. Three of his pictures, however—all painted in different periods—create in the female figure a representation of an *exemplum virtutis*, that is, an illustration of exemplary behavior. The first is the *Young Woman with a Water Pitcher* (The Metropolitan Museum of Art, New York), painted between 1662 and 1665. The protagonist is a middle-class matron, but one who enjoys a higher social position than *The Kitchen Maid*, as we can tell from her clothes and especially the precious, gilded jug she holds in her left hand. The pitcher rests in a basin that sits on a valuable oriental carpet covering the table. Some scholars have associated the pitcher with the only thing Maria Thins left her daughter Catharina. The woman in the picture is caught in a timeless moment—her gaze is lowered and she seems to be reflecting on the pattern of the leaded panes in the window, which, although it is hard to make out, is also decorated with an allegorical figure of Temperance. The pearl-studded jewelry box on the table might here signify vanity and coquetry. In any case an attempt to interpret the picture is suspended, just as the image is, and it is difficult to distinguish the single narrative threads. The woman's expression communicates a sense of tranquility and inner peace, reinforced by the simple frame created by the geometric forms around her. The moment that Vermeer represents is a lasting one; it does not pass, and his harmonies of light, color, and form add further meaning to it. A map of the Seventeen Provinces hangs on the wall behind the woman. It is a valuable object associated with bourgeois homes. All we can see of this map are the southern provinces, which poses another question that is impossible to answer. An early-twentieth-century journalist summed up the painting's intrinsic value succinctly, "*The Young Woman with a Water Pitcher* is one of the immortal products of Dutch art, a gem of the purest serenity." The other two works that offer themselves as *exempla virtuti* are *The Kitchen Maid and The Lace Maker* (Louvre Museum, Paris). The latter was painted in the artist's late phase, between 1669 and 1671.

Vermeer also represented women at their toilette, a genre very much in vogue in Holland at that time. Yet here, too, the artist's interpretation of this subject is unlike any other's before him, affirming again his ability to suggest an elusiveness of meaning in his genre pictures. This is true of the *Woman with a Pearl Necklace* (Staatliche Museen, Gemäldegalerie, Berlin), which was painted about 1664 to 1665. The painter has represented a woman standing in front of a mirror holding up the pearl necklace she wears around her neck. There is a glimpse of the seemingly ubiquitous leaded-glass window on the left; it allows a ray of light, paler than usual, to enter the space. The room is thus enveloped in

Opposite, with details on the following pages:
Johannes Vermeer
Young Woman with a Water Pitcher
1662–1665, oil on canvas
1.5 x 1.3 ft. (45.7 x 40.5 cm)
The Metropolitan Museum of Art, New York

an almost glowing, golden light that creates a masterful harmony of colors, especially in the yellow satin jacket trimmed with ermine that the woman wears. This piece of clothing, which also appears in other works, may have belonged to Catharina; her husband used it to dress some models for his compositions. The intensity of the illumination is ideal to heighten the delicate splendor of the necklace. Here again the woman's simple gesture is frozen, as if she were looking in a mirror for the first time; it is an example of the artist's mastery in representing a particular state of mind with subtle intuition. This does not preclude interpreting the sometimes contradictory, symbolic significance of the numerous objects in the painting. The general tendency among scholars is to see this work as moral counsel, and they thus assign a negative meaning to the mirror and the pearl necklace: the mirror is interpreted as a symbol of vanity, as are the powder puff on the table and the pearls themselves. Often, in fact, personifications of Vanity are portrayed taking a pearl necklace from a jewelry case. The letter lying on the table has been associated with the same theme; it is interpreted as a veiled indication of the lover for whom the woman is primping. The ambiguity of the symbolic meanings of these objects, however, also allows for the opposite reading. The mirror can represent self-awareness and faith, as when it is used as an attribute for Prudence and Truth in Cesare Ripa's *Iconologia*. This text, published in Holland in 1644 (the Italian edition came out in 1593), constituted an important iconographical source for painters in this period. The perfect white sheen of the pearls, for example, could be associated with faith, purity, and virginity. In any case, all of this uncertainty confirms Vermeer's resistance to giving his canvases explicit themes; he preferred to communicate his ideas through the overall atmosphere of the scenes. Scholars who assign a more positive value to the precious objects here in turn suggest that the pearls, the mirror, and the woman's gesture itself express a sense of simplicity, purity, and completeness. This reading is sustained by the several changes Vermeer made to the composition as he painted the scene: it appears that he at first included a musical instrument on the chair in the foreground and a map on the wall behind the figure. By painting them out, Vermeer may have wanted to avoid any negative interpretation of the picture that those two objects could have suggested—musical instruments were often used as references to sensual love, while maps were symbolic of the physical world.

The pearls in this painting are the key to interpreting two other extraordinary pictures executed at about the same time, between 1664 and 1665. They are the *Woman Holding a Balance* (National Gallery of Art, Washington, D.C.) and the *Girl with the Pearl Earring* (Mauritshuis, The Hague). The former represents one of Vermeer's darkest interiors; the weak light that penetrates through the window set high on the left side of the room divides the painting into areas of

Johannes Vermeer
Woman with a Pearl Necklace
1664–1665, oil on canvas
1.8 x 1.5 ft. (55 x 45 cm)
Staatliche Museen, Gemäldegalerie, Berlin

Giovanni Bellini
Allegory of the Prudence of Truth
Early sixteenth century
Gallerie dell'Accademia, Venice

Opposite, with details on the following pages:
Johannes Vermeer
Woman Holding a Balance
1664–1665, oil on canvas
1.4 x 1.2 ft. (42.5 x 38 cm)
National Gallery of Art, Washington, D.C.

light and shadow and illuminates the figure of the young woman. She is trying to balance a scale held delicately in her right hand while she rests her left hand on the table, almost as if to help her concentrate and find a sense of equilibrium. The shadows in the left foreground obliterate everything except for the glowing pearls peeking out of the jewelry box. As in the *Young Woman with a Pitcher of Water*, the protagonist here is also a woman in a domestic interior who is absorbed in her own thoughts. And again there are a variety of different interpretations of this scene. The scale is the focal point of the work's principal theme, and it leads us to further allegorical and philosophical interpretations. These different readings of the picture have also influenced what it has been called over time. It was described, for example, in the catalogue for the 1696 auction in Amsterdam as "a young woman who weighs gold, in a container, by J. Van der Meer of Delft, painted in an extraordinarily artistic and vigorous way." People have generally thought that the scales contained gold or pearls (and hence the title *The Gold Weigher or The Pearl Weigher*). More recently a scholar has demonstrated, by careful analysis of the way in which Vermeer had painted the sheen of pearls and gold, that the scale pans are empty. Other experts have suggested that the woman in the scene is pregnant, rendering her a symbol of the Virgin Mary interceding for the salvation of humankind. The painting on the wall behind her, a *Last Judgment*, seems to reinforce a theological reading of Vermeer's picture. The *Last Judgment* is probably a work that belonged to Maria Thins; the figure of St. Michael holding a scale to separate the elect from the damned is obscured by the woman standing in front of it. Other scholars have dismissed the notion that the woman is pregnant, suggesting instead that she is dressed in a style then in vogue and pointing out that her blue jacket is the same as the yellow one that belonged to Vermeer's wife. Here it is used again, but its color has changed. And the scale pans may be empty, but there is certainly a jewelry box, strings of pearls, and a gold chain on the table; perhaps they represent the temptations of materialism in counterpoint to the mystical theme of the *Last Judgment* and the empty scale. The pearls themselves can contain a

multiplicity of symbolic meanings, from the purity of the Virgin Mary to the sins of pride and intemperance. It is hard, too, not to sense the feeling of peace and inner tranquility emanating from the woman who concentrates so intently on the delicate instrument she is holding. This appears in contrast to the psychological tension suggested by her actions and the implications of the scene on the wall behind her. Perhaps, then, the picture means to associate the eternity of Christ's judgments with the temporality of the woman's, especially given the thoughtful way in which she gazes at the balance. Both are acts of judgment, although the results are quite different in each case. Nonetheless, both decisions must be made carefully, just as the woman does, concentrating all her attention to balance the scale pans perfectly. The essential message of the *Woman Holding a Balance*, whether or not a specifically religious reference is intended, seems to be that life should be lived with temperance and equilibrium. The scale, an attribute of Justice but also of the Last Judgment, symbolizes the woman's responsibility in weighing her own actions, while the mirror located on the wall in front of her indicates the necessity of knowing oneself. Everything in the picture communicates tranquility and harmony, including the skillful play of vertical and horizontal lines, solids and voids, light and shadow, which in their juxtaposition give life to a perfectly balanced yet never static composition. Nor does the painting deliver a single, obvious message; instead Vermeer again chooses only to suggest his theme, using the atmosphere of the scene as a whole to portray a reflective moment that seems suspended and almost frozen in time. This kind of immobility dominates Vermeer's work in the middle years of his career. These compositions, which appear almost repetitive, focus on an isolated figure absorbed in some activity while isolated in a domestic interior that is always seen from the same vantage point.

Different meanings are often hidden behind these compositional similarities, however. This is true, for example, of the *Woman Reading a Letter* (Rijksmuseum, Amsterdam), executed between 1662 and 1664. It returns to the motif of a letter, a subject that will reappear in several of Vermeer's later works. According to some scholars, this picture represents the artist's most complicated juxtaposition of setting and emotional content. There is no way that a simple description of the subject—a woman wearing a blue jacket reading a letter by a window—can suggest even the smallest degree of the image's intensity. Instead, the emotional charge emanating from the woman is communicated by her surroundings, or better, by the way in which the painter has built the space around her. The scene is constructed using a rigid geometry, and it clashes with the apparent "everyday" quality of the interior. This contrast creates a context of mysterious unreality. This is additionally true because the woman is placed at the exact center of the composition,

Opposite, with detail
on the following pages:
Johannes Vermeer
**Girl with the
Pearl Earring**
1664–1665, oil on canvas
1.4 x 1.3 ft. (44.5 x 39 cm)
Mauritshuis, The Hague

GIRL WITH THE PEARL EARRING

Critical enthusiasm for the *Girl with the Pearl Earring* has led to its nickname as the "Mona Lisa of the North," identifying in this portrait a sense of the enigmatic similar to that of Leonardo da Vinci's masterpiece. In a certain sense we can imagine that Vermeer borrowed from the Renaissance master the expedient of placing the figure against a plain, dark ground in such a way that it creates a strong sense of plasticity and highlights her psychological presence. The *Girl with the Pearl Earring* is seen in profile, her mouth open a little, as she turns her head to look at the viewer, exciting a mixed and mysterious sense of attraction. That she seems to appear from the darkness makes her something of a vision that belongs to no specific time or place. Her skin is perfect and smooth, as are the surfaces of the large, dangling pearl earring and the blue turban from which a bit of brilliant yellow cloth hangs, bringing something of the fascination of the exotic to the picture. Some have suggested that Vermeer might have been influenced by an interest in Eastern philosophy that was prevalent at the time in Holland, disseminated through the ties between Dutch settlers in the East Indies and their homeland. It is very likely that many of the art collections in Delft included objects made in Indonesia, strongly steeped in Buddhist and Indian spirituality from which the painter might have taken some sense of absolute stillness and deep psychological introspection. His figures are characterized by a silence and sort of impassivity that expresses more than gestures can, almost as if they were looking for some abstract and elusive interior channel of communication.

Beyond interpretations that can risk being misleading, the *Girl with the Pearl Earring* is a masterpiece of pictorial touch. To define the flesh of her face, Vermeer's brushstrokes at times take the form of the subtle layering of almost transparent glazes, while elsewhere small glimmers of light make her eyes and lips shine. The ensemble of characteristics that define the young woman places her in an absolutely temporal dimension, but it is impossible to place her in any identifiable context or period, and no particular attributes suggest that she is meant to be an allegory or some metaphorical image of anything specific. Perhaps it is this very lack of the specific that allows her to communicate a sense of profound immediacy to the viewer. In this work Vermeer has created a psychological portrait, the charm of which consists most likely in its being an image-symbol that resists any precise identification or definitive interpretation, to become a pure evocation of eternal feminine fascination.

In 1908 the art writer Jan Veth defined the allure of this painting in one simple sentence, "One might say that this work, more than any other Vermeer, was painted with pearl dust." This pearl is both the indecipherable protagonist of the image and the means by which Vermeer "crystallized" his subject. Without it the portrait would stiffen into a static and uncommunicative pose. The appeal of the *Girl with the Pearl Earring* has remained unchanged through time—or perhaps it is strengthened by its passing. This fascination is so strong that it has stimulated contemporary literature, which has made it the fulcrum of equally evasive and enigmatic narrative adventures.

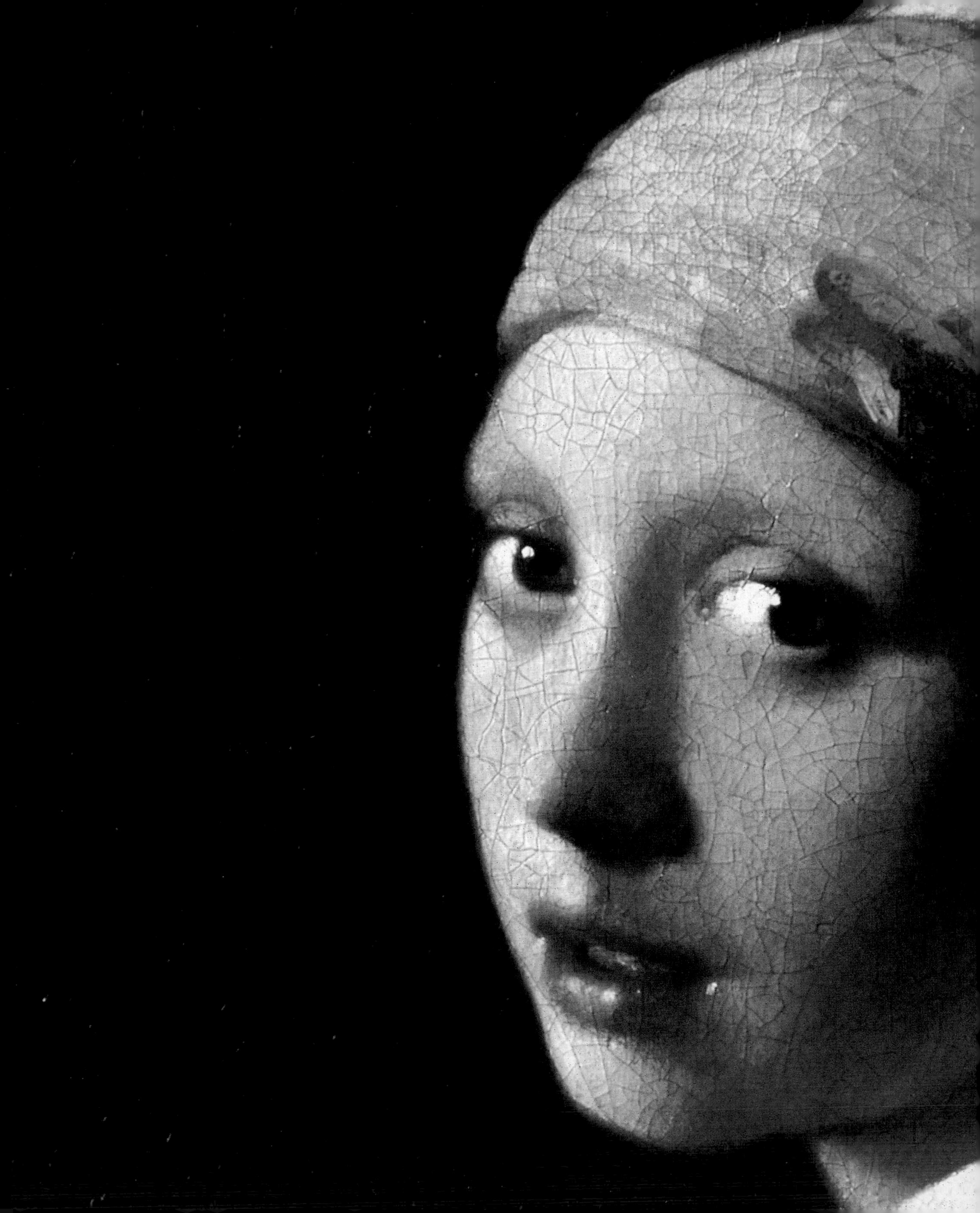

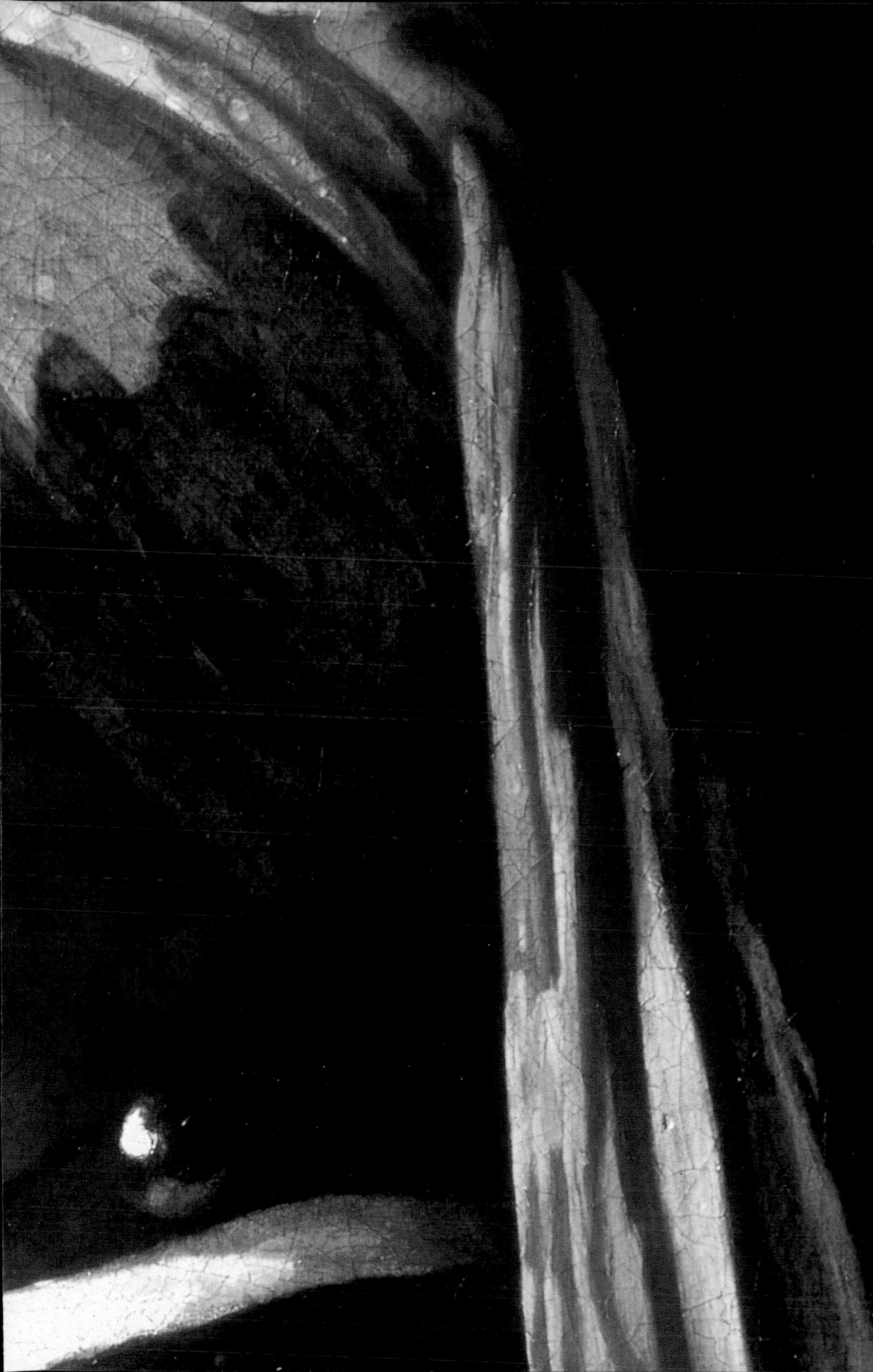

between the table and chair in the foreground. These elements, including the second chair set against the wall, seem practically to enclose the figure in space. Her hands, furthermore, appear visually to be propped up by the horizontal line of the iron rod at the bottom of the map on the wall behind her. Everything in the picture, in fact, seems to eliminate any impression of physical movement, and this is especially true of the careful geometric structure of the composition. Yet Vermeer also knew how to soften the rigidity of the whole by using the snaking lines of the map behind her to suggest the woman's emotional intensity. The same map appears in the *Officer and Laughing Girl*. Made by Balthasar Florisz van Berckenrode in 1620 and published a few years later by Willem Jansz Blaeu, it has been identified as representing Holland and the West Frisian Islands; yet the map looks completely different in the two paintings. In the earlier work, done in 1656 to 1657, the ground is painted a cerulean blue, while in this picture there is an even ochre tone across the entire composition. If the map had been painted blue in the *Woman Reading a Letter*, the blue dress would have receded into the background and the figure of the young woman would have lost its weight and volume.

The X-ray of the painting shows that Vermeer made various modifications to the composition as he worked on it; he extended the map to the left, for example. More significantly, though, he changed the figure's clothing, perhaps to make her more statuesque. Here we again witness the artist's skillful reinforcing of the emotional impact of his composition with the masterful use of color, light, and perspective, all elements that give the scene a strongly reflexive atmosphere. An example is the extraordinary decision to have the light hit the map in a way that concentrates attention on the contrast between the ray of light and the woman's blue dress. The reflective quality of the work is tied to the letter. It provokes a sense of expectation in the woman, revealed by her slightly bowed neck, her slightly open lips, and her slightly raised arms. Vermeer does not reveal the contents of the letter, but he does give us a series of clues that help us interpret the woman's emotional state. Perhaps the map and the empty chair refer to a loved one who is far away, while the fact that the woman interrupted her toilette to read the letter suggests its arrival was unexpected. The faces of the figures in Vermeer's pictures are closed to the viewer; the artist is not interested in telling their stories but prefers to allude to them without invading their privacy or revealing their intimate secrets.

In this phase of his career Vermeer often emphasizes the foreground in his works based on the rules derived from the frequent use contemporary artists made of optical cameras and inverted telescopes. These instruments offered artists useful tools, especially for creating interior scenes and landscapes, and

Opposite, with detail on the following pages:
Johannes Vermeer
Woman Reading a Letter
1662–1664, oil on canvas
1.5 x 1.3 ft. (46.5 x 39 cm)
Rijksmuseum, Amsterdam

many scholars consider it quite likely that Vermeer, too, used them in his own work. The camera obscura, introduced in Holland in 1622, was in its most primitive version just a box with a small hole in its front side and a piece of opaque glass within. The glass reflected the light, and the image at which the box was pointed appeared on it, although upside down. The instrument was refined by adding a lens over the hole, rendering the image clearer and brighter. The telescope solved the problem of the upside-down image that the camera obscura produced, turning it into a direct, if virtual, image. Many of the special optical and luminous effects in Vermeer's paintings can be attributed to the use of these tools. These effects were, however, always subordinate to the final result the artist wanted—and knew he wanted from the beginning.

Vermeer painted two landscapes, both proving his extraordinary ability to "manipulate" reality pictorially. They are *The Little Street*, of about 1658 (Rijksmuseum, Amsterdam), and the *View of Delft*, dated to 1660 or 1661 (Mauritshuis, The Hague). Like his pictures of contemporary interiors, Vermeer's landscapes placed him in a popular artistic current in seventeenth-century Holland, which included specialist painters like Saenredam, Van Ruisdael, Van Goyen, and Van der Heyden. Yet Vermeer was not interested in landscape as a particular view of a city or an atmospheric effect, but rather as the context in which people lived their lives. The figures in his landscapes are small, and at

Jacob van Ruisdael
View of Haarlem
ca. 1670–1675
Mauritshuis,
The Hague

Jan van der Heyden
Church at Veere
1650–1700
Mauritshuis,
The Hague

first glance they seem unimportant details. A more careful analysis will reveal, however, that the landscape itself is "measured" through these tiny figures.

The Little Street is a small and intimate work. It expresses the atmosphere of Vermeer's Delft, with its quiet streets and picturesque buildings, where the sense of community pervades the inhabitants. The artist represented part of two sixteenth-century buildings parallel to the street that runs horizontal to the foreground of the picture. They are united by a wall with doors that lead by way of passageways to interior courtyards. The few people present are surrounded by a visually articulate scene consisting of the red bricks of the facades, the wooden doors and lintels, and the small, leaded-glass windows. This small section of reality is animated by a woman seated on her threshold doing needlepoint, a busy maid in the passageway, and two children kneeling on the sidewalk playing. In truth, though, this scene is less about a fragment of the city of Delft than the poetic beauty of its daily life. The picture has no real temporal or spatial context, and none of the buildings can be easily identified. Furthermore, the opaque light of the cloudy day makes it impossible to say what time of day is represented. Vermeer's scene is suspended outside of time. Like the women represented in his interior scenes, the figures here are anonymous, functioning to communicate an ideal of domestic virtue. Vermeer demonstrates his perfect pictorial technique in *The Little Street*, where he suggested the physical presence

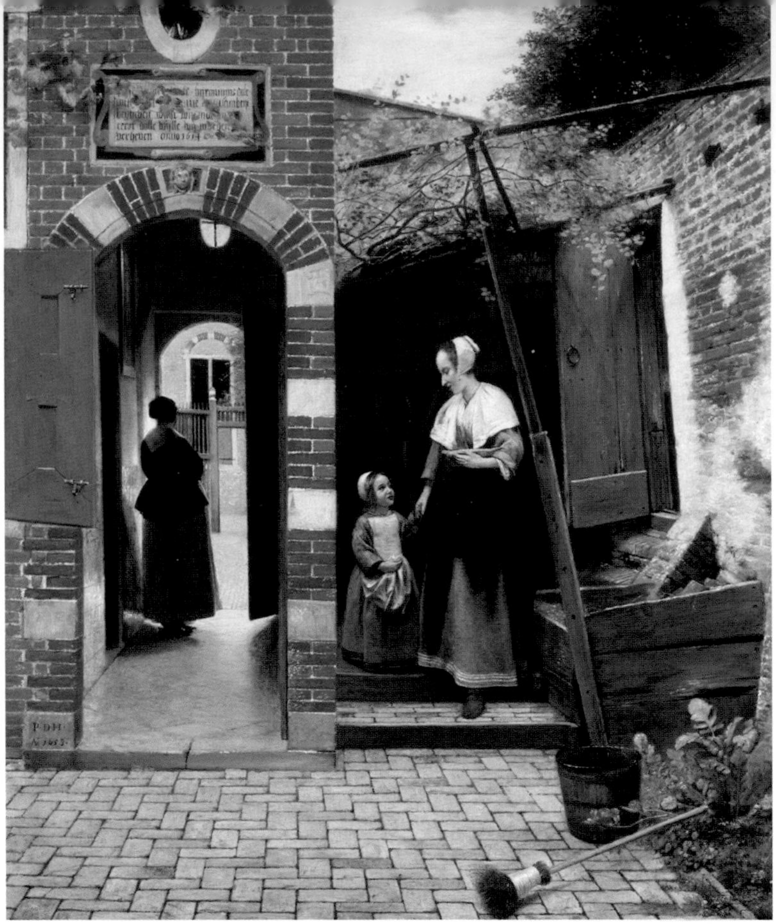

of the buildings in a synthetic way. Furthermore, his skillfully modulated colors build a whole that guides our eye as we look at the composition. The artist seems to want to re-create the atmosphere of the street, not by a careful description of its details so much as by a willingness to adapt some of its architectural elements to his compositional needs. His careful observation of reality is still the principal source for the image, but Vermeer also felt free to combine structures that were actually some distance apart, responding to his need to touch another dimension—the sense of intimacy and stability inherent in domestic virtue. There are many similarities to De Hooch's *The Courtyard of a House in Delft* (1658, National Gallery, London), in which the painter represents a slice of domestic life set in an open courtyard. The subtle narrative thread in De Hooch's picture gives way in *The Little Street* to a discreet and silent spirituality.

There are no documents that prove Vermeer used a camera obscura, but the hypothesis that he did is strengthened by his *View of Delft*, a painting in which the artist was more interested in clarity and simplicity than a pure realism. This picture is a rather free and lyrical interpretation of the city, painted from the south and looking toward the port that connected it to Rotterdam. Some of the buildings represented are still recognizable—including the Rotterdam Gate, with its two small, conical towers depicted on the right side of the composition

Pieter de Hooch
The Courtyard of a House in Delft
1658
National Gallery, London

Opposite, with detail on the following pages:
Johannes Vermeer
The Little Street
ca. 1658, oil on canvas
1.8 x 1.4 ft.
(54.3 x 44 cm)
Rijksmuseum, Amsterdam

Left, with detail on
the following pages:
Johannes Vermeer
View of Delft
1660–1661, oil on canvas
3.2 x 3.9 ft.
(98.5 x 118.5 cm)
Mauritshuis,
The Hague

and probably painted from a sketch made onsite. The figures in this scene are among the most innovative aspects of the work. Like those in *The Little Street*, they are simple human presences and are not meant to express commercial or other specific activity in the city. Here again Vermeer preferred to place his architectural elements parallel to the picture plane; his faithful adherence to the principles of orthogonal composition distinguishes him from his contemporaries, whose urban views were more fragmentary. Uniformity was important to Vermeer, and he created an overall tonality in which gradations of ochres and browns dominate but are animated here and there with strokes of red and yellow paint. Light is also fundamentally important; it illuminates the landscape with varied intensity, leaving some buildings in shadow. The part of the city in the background is flooded with intense sunlight, while the advancing dark clouds throw a shadow over the foreground. This manipulation of light is one of the novelties Vermeer introduced to the tradition of landscape painting, the other being his desire to move beyond descriptive realism, to create an atmosphere that somehow expresses the city's character and history. Some of the optical effects in the *View of Delft* derive from the use of a camera obscura; they include the reflections on the water, the refracted light, and the imprecision of the painted surfaces. Vermeer created these effects with miniscule brushstrokes that deny any weightiness and create instead a sense of immateriality. It is not documented whether Vermeer actually used optical tools here, but it remains a plausible hypothesis because there is a house across from the port from which the painter might have used a camera obscura to achieve a similar effect to what we see in the picture. Even if the artist had used such a tool, his purpose was not to obtain a "perfect" view, but rather to create special effects and to exalt the sensation of reality by accenting the contrasts between light and dark and making the colors more vivid. To achieve this, Vermeer modified the optical effects by drawing on what he really saw. The lack of focus in this image is the result of his skillful pictorial remaking of the slice of reality framed here. The dimensions of the buildings as well as their placement and reflections in the water are manipulated to make the picture represent more than mere topography. On the one hand Vermeer's pictorial technique makes Delft's presence almost tangible, while on the other the city itself becomes abstract and immaterial. It is there to be admired, but at a distance because one cannot actually approach Delft from the vantage point Vermeer chose. Instead, he "re-created" it according to his interior eye. The picture is enriched by a strong sense of symbolism coming from the light that suggests the vitality of the small city. *The Little Street* and *View of Delft* belong to the group of paintings that collector Van Ruijven acquired from Vermeer in 1665, later sold at auction in 1696.

Johannes Vermeer
Study of a Young Woman
1665–1667, oil on canvas
1.5 x 1.3 ft. (45 x 40 cm)
The Metropolitan Museum of Art, New York

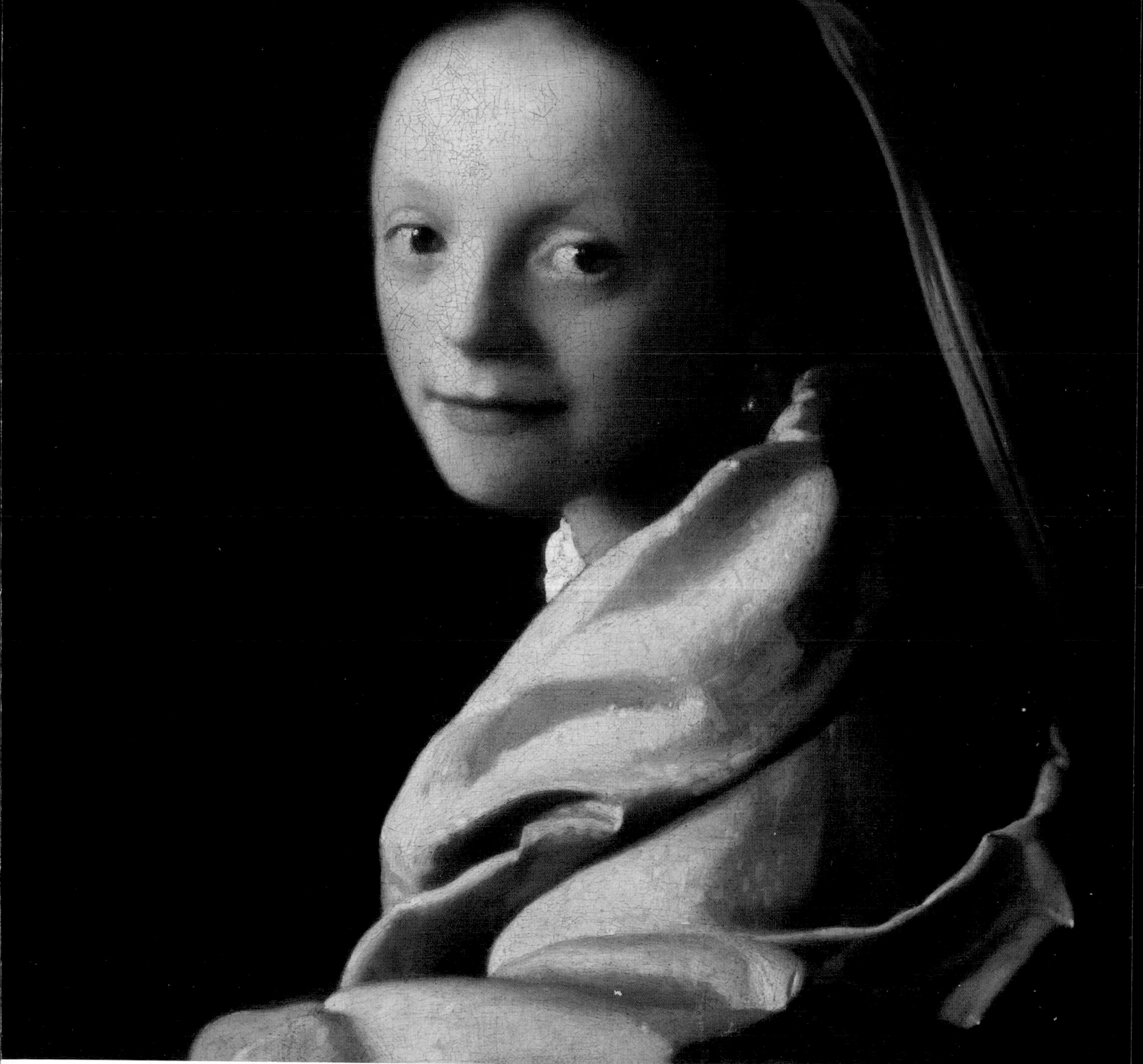

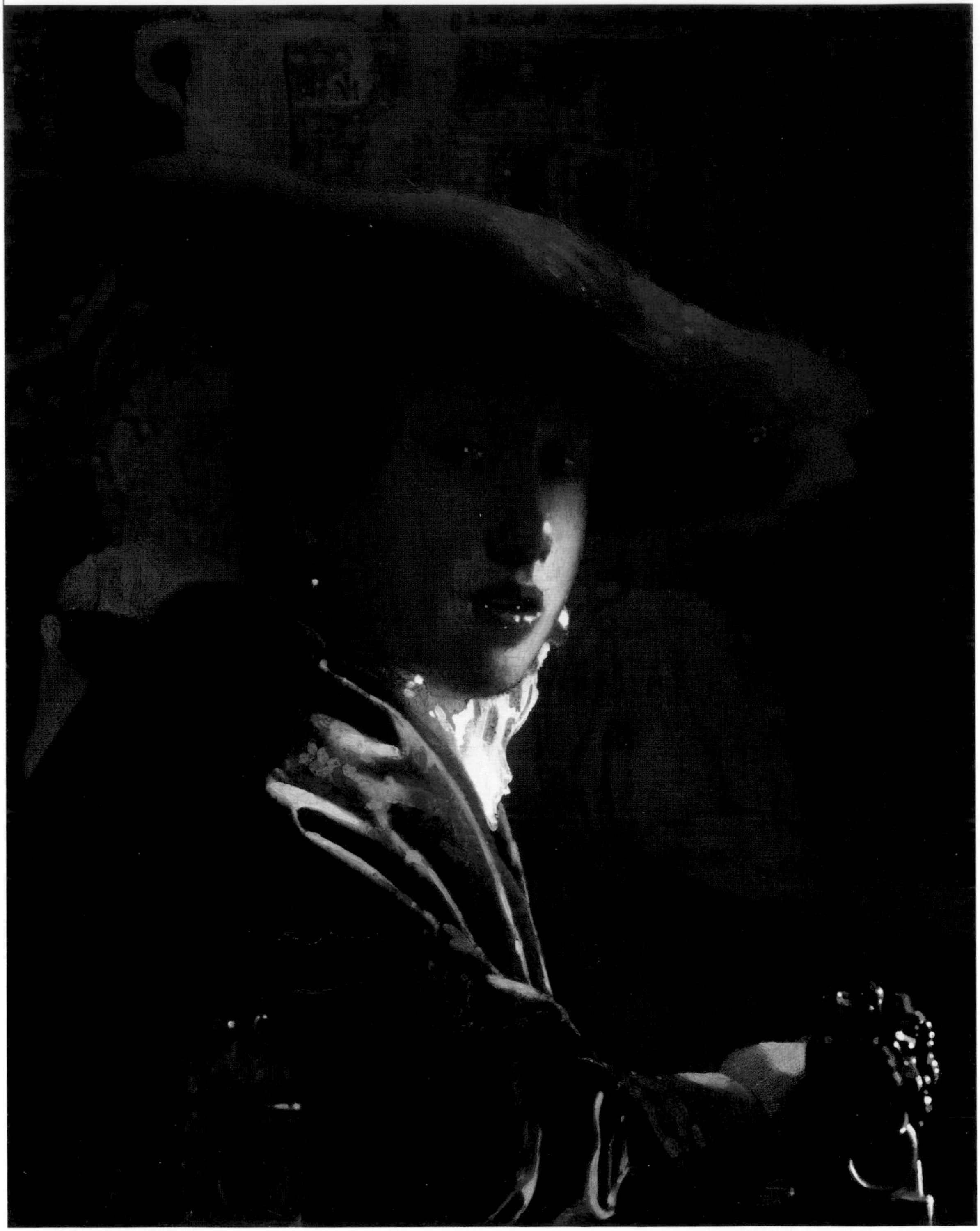

At the same time of his landscapes Vermeer continued to paint interior scenes, the horizons of which are the walls of the rooms that contain them. He also painted several portraits of a single female figure emerging from a dark background into the foreground. Three of them are related to the *Girl with the Pearl Earring*: the *Study of a Young Woman* (1665–1667, The Metropolitan Museum of Art, New York); *Girl with the Red Hat* (ca.1665, National Gallery of Art, Washington, D.C.); and *Girl with a Flute* (National Gallery of Art, Washington, D.C.), the date of which is debated—it is either 1665 or 1667. The first depicts a young woman in a gray dress whom some scholars have identified as Mary, Vermeer's oldest daughter. Many of the characteristics of this work are similar to that of the *Girl with the Pearl Earring*, including the earring itself, which has the same ambiguous meaning, although here it has a more discreet shape. The figure's position is comparable; we see her from the side, but she turns her head to look at us. Her hair is pulled back and braided under the veil (which indicates that she is married). The attribution of the other two portraits to Vermeer is still debated, however, and some scholars argue that his signatures on them were added later.

The scholars who reject Vermeer's authorship of the *Girl with the Red Hat* do so because they believe its style, composition, and color are unlike other works he executed in this period. The fact that it is painted on panel rather than canvas, the support for all of Vermeer's other pictures, feeds these doubts. Other scholars, however, hold the opposite opinion, suggesting that the artist used a camera obscura in painting the portrait. As evidence they point to the passages of pointillist technique, especially in the reflections of light on the lion-head knobs of the armchair and in the folds of the woman's dress. The highlights on her dress were created with dabs of yellow paint to contrast with the blue, the dress itself painted over a reddish-brown ground to give greater depth to the color. (The camera obscura would have been used here, as it was before, for the detailed finishing touches.) The presence of strong colors is concentrated in two distinct areas, the dress and the hat. The brilliant red of the latter intensifies the immediacy of the woman's gaze and activates a sense of psychological presence. The cool blue of the dress, in contrast, gives the impression of a recession toward the back of the picture. The light falls diagonally across the hat so that its ample brim casts a shadow over a large part of the woman's face. Her eyes, the focal point of a face, are left intentionally in that shadow; Vermeer here appears influenced by the principle of "dissimulation," according to which a figure's emotions must be masked to increase the viewer's curiosity.

Attributed to
Johannes Vermeer
Girl with the Red Hat
ca. 1665, oil on panel
9 x 7 in. (23 x 18 cm)
National Gallery of Art,
Washington, D.C.

The X-ray of the painting revealed that the panel was reused; another painter had employed it before for the bust-length portrait of a man, which is upside-down with respect to the woman. Fabritius's name has been associated with the first image, but the question of who indeed painted it seems destined to remain unsolved.

The third portrait, the *Girl with a Flute*, which is also on panel, has been the subject of even greater debate. Its support has suggested to those who believe it is by Vermeer that it is a pendant piece to the *Girl with the Red Hat*. Uncertainty over its attribution, though, is rooted in the quality of its execution, which is generally judged to be inferior to Vermeer's masterful technique. The *Girl with a Flute* does have many similarities to the *Girl with the Red Hat*, from the proportions of the sitter to the fact that both young women look at the viewer with attentive glances, their mouths open in an expectant expression. The Asian-style hat in the former also casts a shadow across the woman's eyes, giving her face an aura of mystery. The two paintings do have undeniable differences, however, and they are enough to undermine the theory that they were intended as pendant pieces. The colors in the *Girl with a Flute* appear less vivid and the brushstrokes less fluid. Vermeer, or whoever painted it, made a number of changes to the image after sketching it out; he added the finger resting on the flute, for example, suggesting that the instrument was not part of the original composition. The most widely held opinion is that Vermeer designed the picture and laid it out, perhaps then abandoning it before it was finished. In that case it seems likely that a second artist completed it, perhaps a follower who was trying to remain faithful to the master's style. If this were true, the *Girl with a Flute* would be the only picture we know of that can be attributed to a follower of Vermeer's. It would also explain the lack of the sense of a psychological presence in the young woman that is typical of the master's work. This possibility further suggests that Vermeer had a small circle of followers who would have drawn him out of his isolation.

A few years earlier, in about 1662, the artist added musical instruments to his interior scenes, enriching them with strongly metaphorical implications. Vermeer had already used instruments in some of his earlier works, where they are depicted with such care and precision that it suggests he had admired them in person—a distinct possibility given that he himself was a connoisseur of music. When the artist decided to make music an actor in his pictures, he did it not with images of the public performances of concertos or sonatas, but by depicting private recitals or people playing alone. In its essence, music was considered first and foremost an interior emotion, a suggestion to be enjoyed in solitude and the bearer of symbolic and metaphorical significance. *The Music Lesson* (Royal Collection, Buckingham Palace, London), painted between 1662 and 1665, fits into this category. The relationship between music and love here is very close. The scene is set in an upper-middle-class interior; the figures are

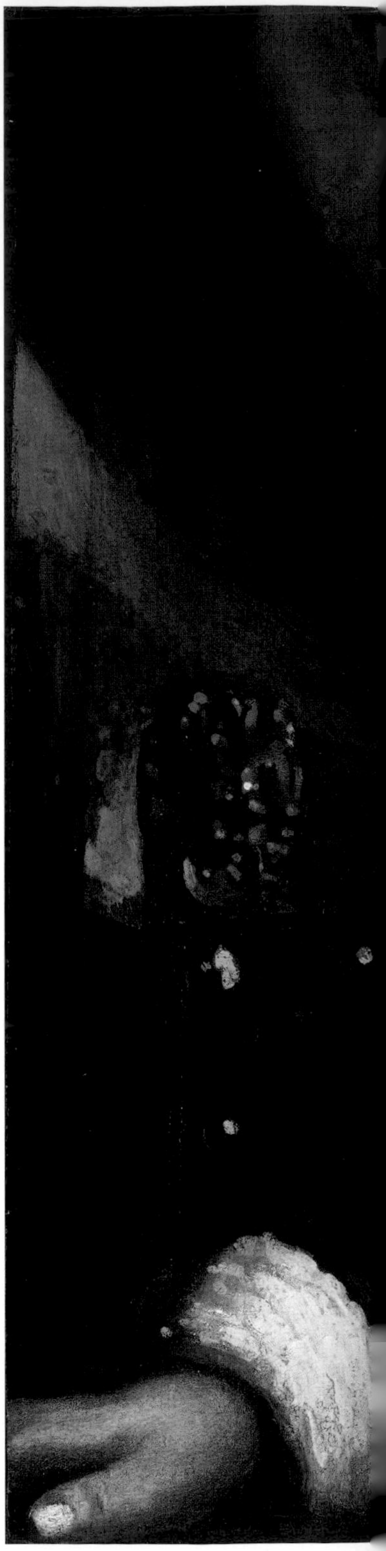

Attributed to
Johannes Vermeer
Girl with a Flute
1665–1667, oil on panel
8 x 7 in. (20.2 x 18 cm)
National Gallery of Art,
Washington, D.C.

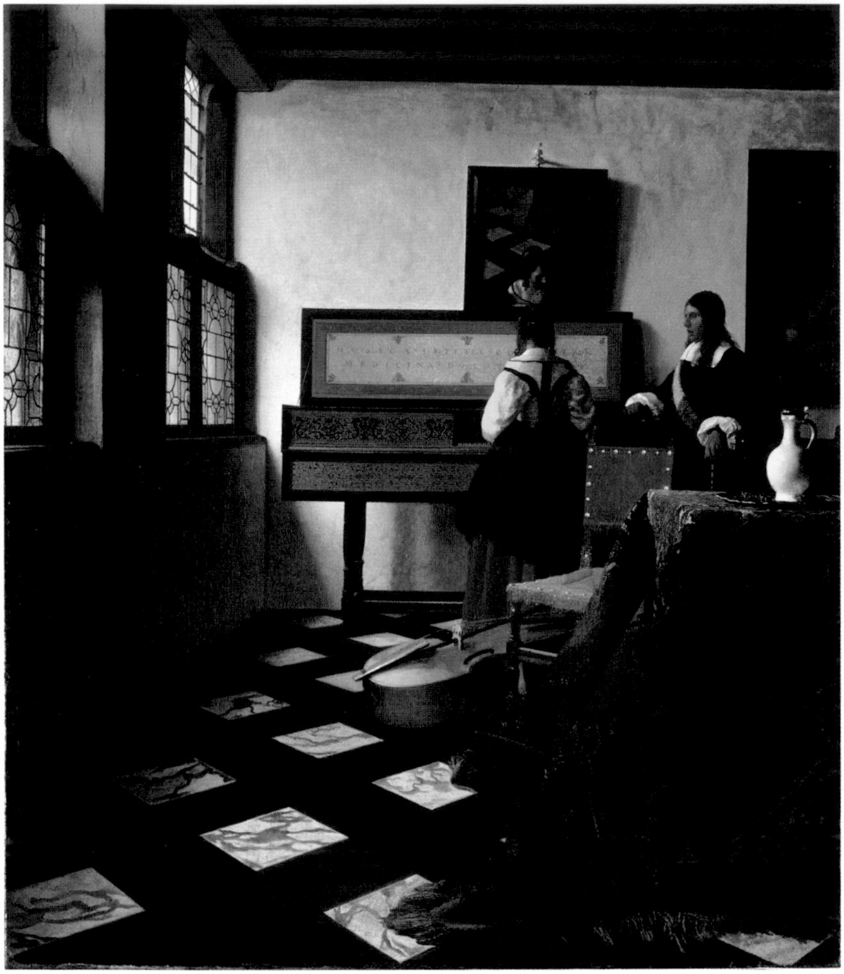

Johannes Vermeer
The Music Lesson
1662–1665, oil on canvas
2.4 x 2.1 ft. (73.5 x 64.1 cm)
Royal Collection,
Buckingham Palace,
London

placed in the background, near the rear wall of the room where a young woman is playing a virginal. Although she stands with her back to the viewer, we can see her face, turned toward the man beside her, in the mirror hanging above the musical instrument. It also reflects the painter of the portrait's easel, placing him, too, within the scene. As one might expect, Vermeer leaves the theme of the image intentionally open, with a variety of possible interpretations suggested by the series of veiled clues that are so skillfully orchestrated in all of his compositions. The scene remains immutably silent, but the delicate melody of the virginal is suggested in the articulation of the composition itself, which appears to reflect the rhythm of the music. The construction of space here—more than in any work thus far considered—is the key element. Vermeer has increased the sense of depth in the picture through the perfect geometry of the floor tiles, and has played with the perspective, inserting multiple points of view by means of the mirror. Many scholars have identified the man standing next to the young woman as her instructor, while others have underscored how the painting focuses on ideas of love, rather than the value of musical instruction in its own right. Once again a possible key to reading the work is provided by the picture painted within the picture, barely visible on the right side of the room. It depicts *Roman Charity*, a work that Vermeer probably borrowed from his mother-in-law. It portrays the story of Pero, who offers to succor her imprisoned and starving father, Cimon, with her own breast. The image represents the ideal of Christian charity, and suggests a daughter's love for her father as conceived in spiritual terms; but it also more generally refers to the comfort and consolation offered through love. In Vermeer's hands musical harmony becomes a metaphor for the harmony of love. The inscription on the virginal's cover further underscores the ability of music to console: MVSICA LETITIAE COMES MEDICINA DOLORVM, or MUSIC IS THE COMPANION OF JOY AND A BALM FOR PAIN. The jug of wine on the table may have a similar symbolic function as a container that brings nourishment. Finally, the cello lying on the floor echoes the euphony of the

Right, with detail on the following pages:
Johannes Vermeer
The Concert
1664–1666, oil on canvas
2.3 x 2 ft. (69.2 x 62.8 cm)
Isabella Stewart Gardner Museum, Boston (stolen in 1990)

virginal, just as two hearts can, even when separated, still beat in perfect harmony. The same value is inherent in the mirror, which binds an object to its reflection—like the music that links the man and woman even though they are physically separated by the chair between them.

The Concert (stolen from the Isabella Stewart Gardener Museum, Boston, in March 1990), painted in more or less the same years (1664–1666), offers a similar reading. The inclusion here of two more paintings within the picture confirms that they are "meaningful presences" in Vermeer's work. These two paintings—a landscape and Van Baburen's *Procuress*—hang on the rear wall of the room. The landscape, which recalls the decoration on the underside of the virginal's lid, is idyllic, and when paired with Van Baburen's work may allude to the excesses music can excite. Vermeer warns us that the only difference between balance of the mind and confusion of the senses is reason and self-control.

Girl Interrupted at Her Music (Frick Collection, New York), another work with a much debated attribution, can be tied to the same moralizing admonition. Dated to about 1660 to 1661, it depicts a young woman who has just put her lute down on the table to read the letter the man has brought her. The young woman's uncertainty—revealed by the way she gazes at something outside the picture—about whether or not to read the letter betrays its amorous content. The painting hanging on the rear wall is another indication of the subject of the missive because it represents a putto or cupid bearing a message of love. In this case music is associated with wine, that "love potion" to which the jug and cup on the table refer. Vermeer here again assigns a variety of metaphorical values to the objects he depicts.

There is some debate, too, over the attribution of *Woman with a Lute* (ca. 1664, The Metropolitan Museum of Art, New York), which shows a young woman distracted from tuning her instrument by a ray of sunlight shining through the window. The effects of the setting and light are extremely delicate; we see them in the reflections on the pearl necklace and earring. The symbolic meaning of the picture focuses on the lute, an instrument with a low range of tones that was well suited for small and intimate spaces.

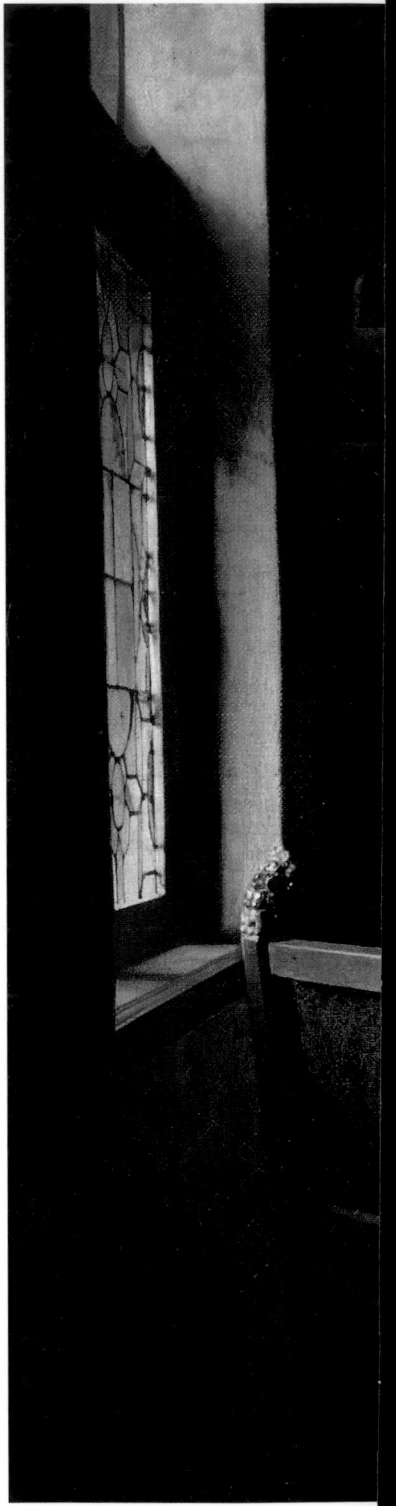

Johannes Vermeer
Girl Interrupted at Her Music
1660–1661, oil on canvas
1.3 x 1.5 ft. (39.4 x 44.5 cm)
The Frick Collection, New York

Johannes Vermeer
Woman with a Lute
1664, oil on canvas
1.7 x 1.5 ft. (52 x 46 cm)
The Metropolitan
Museum of Art,
New York

De Noord

Chapter 3
Symbolism and Science

Holland had reached the peak of its economic and political development early in the 1600s, and signs of the long decline to come first appeared in the middle of the century. The country's commercial successes were the source of continual conflicts with its neighbors, especially France and England, which attacked the Dutch fleet three times—in 1652, 1665, and 1675. These confrontations weakened Holland and put a halt to the expansionist policies that had won it a place on the international stage. This general situation in Holland was reflected in its artistic trends, which moved rather quickly toward an "international" style that favored a return to classicism.

For a little while at least the small city of Delft continued to enjoy one of the most fertile and productive periods in its history. This was in large part due to the development of its famous ceramics industry and the flowering of a particularly lively artistic community. The presence of artists Steen, De Hooch, and Vermeer provided a strong impetus for the representation of everyday subjects, and Delft was, for a few years, a small arts center, a destination for travelers, and a meeting place for collectors and dealers. Vermeer's studio was, at the end of the 1660s, a gathering place for intellectuals and potential patrons, and the artist himself enjoyed some fame, as evidenced in several contemporary travel diaries. Pieter Teding van Berckhout, a wealthy young man of the petty rural nobility, noted in his journal on May 14, 1669: "When we arrived [in Delft] I met an excellent painter called Vermeer who showed me a number of curiosities he had painted." Adding on June 21: "Then I went out to visit the famous painter Vermeer. He showed me some examples of his work which were extraordinary and curious for their perspective." In 1670 Vermeer was nominated for a second time to be dean of the Guild of St. Luke, an indication of the status he had achieved in the local arts community.

In this period the painter continued to produce extraordinary representations of everyday life, and he developed, in particular, numerous variations of pictures focused around letters, a subject he had already

Johannes Vermeer
Allegory of Painting (The Artist's Studio)
(detail)
1666–1667, oil on canvas
4 x 3.3 ft. (120 x 100 cm)
Kunsthistorisches Museum, Vienna

introduced into his work. Now, however, this theme was articulated in somewhat richer compositions that were built around the secret, feminine universe. A lone woman, intent on her writing, or a matron whose maid hands her a mysterious missive are the enigmatic presences in his works—they are anonymous and unidentifiable characters. Vermeer was surrounded in his daily life by women (his mother, wife, mother-in-law, and daughters), yet he did not with any certainty portray them in his pictures, though many have tried valiantly in later times to identify them in his work. It is possible that some of the women in his household served as models or, more simply, as a source of inspiration, but the artist's search for abstract compositions frozen in silent stillness pushed him to strip away any element with an identifiable historical or spatial reference. And despite the fact that they were constructed with objects from his own household, the sets Vermeer created in every one of his interior scenes was transformed into "another" space, as soon as it was painted on his canvas, by the continuous play of symbolic meanings and cross-references.

Vermeer's work from the mid-1660s becomes more tightly executed and his atmosphere more limpid, although the painter did not change his working method and continued to study the construction of each image with extreme care. *A Lady Writing* (ca. 1665, National Gallery of Art, Washington, D.C.) attests to Vermeer's meticulous and time-consuming working method. In the suffused light of an interior, a young woman raises her eyes from the letter she is writing to look at the viewer. She holds a pen in her right hand and in the other a sheet of paper. The interruption seems not to surprise or startle her. She has ribbons in her hair, pearl earrings, and she wears the yellow satin jacket with fur trim that we have seen in other pictures by Vermeer. We catch a glimpse of more pearls beside the inkpot and in a jewelry box, introducing the theme of vanity, very likely one of the keys to understanding the picture. In traditional Dutch painting, a woman writing a letter is normally associated with love, a symbolism that contemporary painters made abundantly clear by inserting explicit references to it in their work. Without abandoning his own propensity for ambiguity, Vermeer himself introduces an element in *A Lady Writing* that refers to an amorous relationship—the painting hanging on the back wall of the room. It depicts a still life with musical instruments in which the theme of music refers to love. Vermeer studied every detail in his composition in order to create a sense of tranquility, including the pose of the figure, the placement of the chair and table, and the painting on the back wall as well as the proportional relationships in the picture and the play of light and shadow, which is both simple and synthetic. Among the great innovations in this work is the

Opposite, with detail
on the following pages:
Johannes Vermeer
A Lady Writing
ca. 1665, oil on canvas
1.5 x 1.2 ft. (45 x 39.9 cm)
National Gallery of Art,
Washington, D.C.

woman's awareness of the presence of an onlooker. Vermeer here modified his compositional formula, which had remained largely unchanged until this moment, and inserted a new variation on the theme of the letter, that is, the arrival of an invisible visitor in the otherwise private room. Even though this element tends automatically to create a sort of narrative, the artist has consigned any physical action to a secondary role, so that we can focus exclusively on the young woman's reflexive posture. The slight smile on her face is the only indication of her reaction to her unexpected visitor, whose arrival has caused neither surprise nor consternation. Some scholars have suggested that this work is an actual portrait, and that for this reason Vermeer focused on the figure to reveal both her physical and her psychological presence. Her facial features are not idealized, and up close they are very similar to those of the figure in the *Study of a Young Woman*, also painted with short, delicate brushstrokes.

Vermeer never used the same iconographic motif or compositional formula without introducing some kind of variation that allowed him to re-create, *ex novo*, his universe of symbols with multiple meanings. This is the case with *Mistress and Maid* (Frick Collection, New York), a picture executed between 1666 and 1668. The novelty here is the servant who comes out of the shadows to give her mistress a letter. The latter wears the same yellow jacket trimmed with ermine fur that we have seen before. The woman herself has just finished writing something on a sheet of paper, and we can read in her a slight hesitation in accepting the proffered letter; Vermeer seems to concentrate on the woman's agitation. There is no hint of whether the letter she has just finished has any relation to the one she has received. There is, however, a distinct relationship between the woman and her maid, established by their exchange of glances, and this introduces another novel element in the painting. The scene focuses on the relationship between the two women, rather than on any single moment of contemplative introspection. Both figures stand in the foreground, strongly illuminated against the dark background from which they emerge. The painter from Delft needed only a few elements to create a simple form—a single gesture and the expression on a partially obscured face communicate all the complexity of emotion in the picture. Even though this painting is constructed with only a few elements, Vermeer chose to make it relatively large.

The more elaborate *The Love Letter* (Rijksmuseum, Amsterdam), however, is painted on a smaller canvas. Executed between 1669 and 1670, this picture revisits the subject of the secret message, with the maid acting as her mistress's confidante. Its small format notwithstanding, the painter demonstrates his mastery of perspective by constructing a complicated series

Opposite, with details on the following pages:
Johannes Vermeer
Mistress and Maid
1666–1668, oil on canvas
3 x 2.6 ft. (89.5 x 78.1 cm)
The Frick Collection, New York

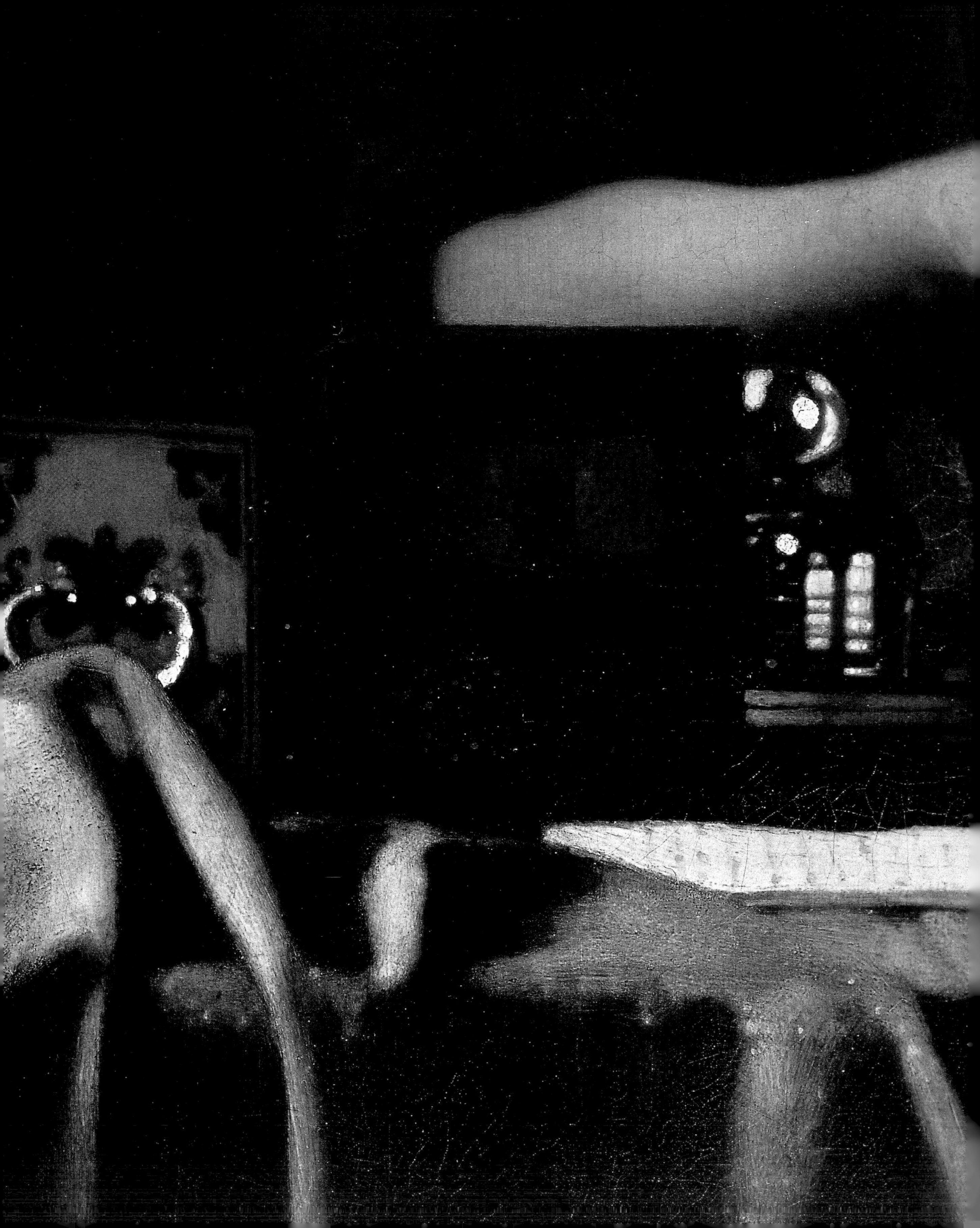

of spaces and creating the impression that the viewer is standing in the dark and disorderly antechamber, looking in on the scene. The raised curtain allows us to see into the brightly lit room where the scene between the two women is playing out. Some scholars have suggested that Vermeer used an inverted telescope to make this painting, given that the viewer stands on the threshold of the room, the dark foreground is depicted in strong relief, and the objects closer to the foreground are the least focused. The mistress, her servant, and the interior they occupy are all sharply defined, even though they tend to retreat into the depth of the picture. Regardless of whether he used any optical tools, Vermeer's skill is obvious in the way he plays with perspective in order to allow the removed viewer to witness this event. The perspective grid represented in the floor tiles leads the spectator's eye to the bright interior, yet its vanishing point is in the dark antechamber, a little above the knob on the back of the chair. The exchange between the two figures remains protected in an intimate space that the viewer is not allowed to enter.

This very carefully constructed perspective system situates Vermeer among a group of contemporary Dutch artists who were especially interested in illusionistic space. The device of viewing a scene through a doorway has a precedent in the artist's youthful *Maid Asleep* (The Metropolitan Museum of Art, New York), and it seems probable that Vermeer took his cue here from De Hooch. Once again, however, the two painters' intentions were very different. While the latter favored narrative, the former concentrated on the psychological implications of his work. In *The Love Letter* the woman's expression seems agitated, and again the focus is on a particularly feminine complicity between the two figures, suggested by their glances and apparently mutual understanding. The reassuring posture of the maid is in contrast to the woman's worry about the contents of the letter, and the maid's confidence is reinforced by the seascape hanging on the wall behind her—the calm sea is a good omen for love. The idyllic landscape in the picture above the seascape may have the same meaning, while the basket of linens, the petit-point cushion on the floor, and the broom near the door allude to the domestic activities that the women ignore as they are distracted by the thoughts of love suggested by the silenced mandolin. Vermeer further complicated the meaning here by seeming to suggest that behind the stability of the scene there is an anxiety that springs from the uncertainty of emotion. In this sense his closed construction of space metaphorically reinforces the contrast between external appearances, which are measured and measurable, and the inner world of feeling that, like sea travel, is often subjected to the danger of shipwreck.

Opposite, with details on the following pages:
Johannes Vermeer
The Love Letter
1669–1670, oil on canvas
1.4 x 1.3 ft. (44 x 38.5 cm)
Rijksmuseum,
Amsterdam

Opposite, with details
on the following pages:
Johannes Vermeer
Allegory of Painting
(The Artist's Studio)
1666–1667, oil on canvas
4 x 3.3 ft. (120 x 100 cm)
Kunsthistorisches
Museum, Vienna

ALLEGORY OF PAINTING (THE ARTIST'S STUDIO)

Although there is no single work in Vermeer's oeuvre that represents all of his poetry and style, it is very tempting to see the *Allegory of Painting* as one of the few windows we have into the mysterious world of the "Sphinx of Delft." Begun in about 1666 and, according to some, not completed until 1673, the painting certainly represents the personal and artistic world of the painter, condensed into an image with an extremely complex allegorical meaning. We need to be very careful of any iconographic interpretation of the work that sees meaning in the individual objects represented lest we muddy the magical quiet of the light, which is the real protagonist of the picture. As the light enters from the left, it slips along the rear wall of the room, curls through the ripples of the map, and then it reveals, one by one, the details that make the small space of the studio so dense with significance. We view Vermeer from behind as he paints the young woman, who is posing in classical dress. Her attitude recalls that of a muse, an identification that is reinforced by the atmosphere around her—a profound silence, abstract beauty, and contemplation that translates into action.

The fact that the artist saw this painting as a sort of personal manifesto is confirmed by his desire not to sell it and to keep it for himself—a task at which he was successful for the ten years before he died. His widow as well did everything she could after his death to keep it, although she was forced to part with the painting in 1676 to settle some debts. According to a notarial act dated February 24, Catharina Bolnes gave her mother, Maria Thins, "a painting done…by her late husband which depicts the art of painting." Catharina's intentions were to keep the picture as safe from her creditors as she possibly could, but only a year later the executor of Vermeer's estate decided to put it up for auction regardless.

The title of the painting, which only vaguely refers to the iconographical information it contains, was chosen not by the artist but by laymen, who probably altered the true allegorical meaning of the figure of the woman. The model wears a laurel wreath on her head and carries a trumpet in her right hand and a book in her left, and thus it seems does not personify Painting but instead Clio, the Muse of History. The drapery drawn back like a theater curtain across the left side of the picture appears to separate reality from fiction. Vermeer was inspired by Cesare Ripa's *Iconologia*, which had been translated into Dutch by Dirk Pers in 1644, confirming the picture as an allegory of history, not painting. The book the woman holds refers to the presence of the past, that is, to history. Her laurel wreath that the artist is painting with bluish reflections on his canvas is an attribute of Fame, as is the trumpet she holds in her right hand. The plaster mask on the table refers to art as fiction. The figure of the artist, seen from behind (and thus remaining anonymous), is seated on a stool in front of his easel, occupying a central position in the composition. The detail of the empty canvas on which he is painting the laurel wreath gives it the meaning it had in the Renaissance, when it was interpreted as a symbol of the idea. In this sense the wreath becomes an icon of the artistic concept, which assumes a material form only when the artist paints it.

The complexity and power of the subject matter notwithstanding, Vermeer has stripped away any suggestion of rhetoric and other pompous resonances by representing the artist seated comfortably, with his legs apart and his hose loosened, once again setting the scene in a room in his own house, as we can guess from the flooring and other objects we have seen before. Clio, therefore, celebrates the glory of the artist by the value of history, but many other details allow us to suggest further interpretations that must remain unresolved. One example is the mask lying on the table, which some scholars think might refer to the rivalry between the arts first posed by Leonardo and resolved here by Vermeer, who declares the superiority of painting. The model's lowered gaze also has no single, definitive explanation, because it can relate to the book, the map behind her, or the reciprocal relationship among all these objects. Another reading suggests that the painting is an allegorical celebration of specific historical events. A particular interpretation of the big map on the wall points, for instance, to a discreet homage to the House of Orange and its military victories. In any case, the difficulties of interpretation should not distract us from the grandeur of the masterpiece itself. Here in his mature period Vermeer was able to transform exact description into abstraction and transcendent emotion.

The *Allegory of Painting* (Kunsthistorisches Museum, Vienna)—also known as *The Artist's Studio*—offers an even more careful articulation of perspective. It is dated from 1666 to 1667 and is generally considered a sort of "manifesto" of Vermeer's artistic objectives and style. As Albert Blankert wrote, "No other painting fuses so perfectly a naturalistic technique, a brilliantly illuminated space, and such a complex composition." In representing a painter (himself?) in this work, Vermeer shows that he knows he has achieved some fame and social status; something his peers in the political and cultural life of seventeenth-century Holland also understood. The myth that Vermeer remained an isolated and unknown figure in the Dutch arts scene in the middle of the seventeenth century has no foundation, given that recent studies have revealed his series of highly placed contacts. The most important of them was with Constantijn Huygens, a greatly influential politician and intellectual who dominated Dutch cultural life for part of the seventeenth century. Secretary to the *Stadtholder*, Frederick Henry (1584–1647), it was very likely Huygens who sent both the French diplomat, Balthasar de Monconys, and Pieter Teding van Berckhout to visit Vermeer's studio. The profound bond between Vermeer and his culture is demonstrated by several pictures in which the artist showed a perfect knowledge of scientific instruments and objects. The maps and globes, both terrestrial and celestial, in these paintings are represented with a precision that leads us to assume a direct familiarity with these objects. Like most Dutch people of his time Vermeer traveled little, generally venturing only to places a few kilometers away from Delft or, at most, going all the way to Amsterdam. Yet he had a great admiration for the heroes of the sea and the sailors who had made Holland a great colonial power. National pride was supplemented by a profound interest in science, and the relationship of the latter to painting is one of the most interesting aspects of Dutch culture in the seventeenth century. The best example is René Descartes's arrival in Amsterdam in 1628, an event that provided a strong impetus for the study of both the sciences and philosophy. A large number of popular publications created a market among a relatively open-minded public for treatises on geography, physics, mathematics, astronomy, and medicine. The production of precise instruments provided a significant contribution to the economies of both Delft and Leyden. This embrace of science can be explained, in part, by the effort the United Provinces made to stay current and to find new ways to affirm their recent independence and national identity. Vermeer was very receptive to these cultural stimuli, as we can see in two canvases, sometimes considered pendant pieces: *The Astronomer* (Louvre Museum, Paris) and *The Geographer* (Städelsches Kunstinstitut und Städtische Galerie, Frankfurt). These are the

Johannes Vermeer
The Astronomer (detail)
1668, oil on canvas
1.7 x 1.5 ft. (50.8 x 46.3 cm)
Louvre Museum,
Paris

Opposite, with detail
on the following pages:
Johannes Vermeer
The Astronomer
1668, oil on canvas
1.7 x 1.5 ft. (50.8 x 46.3 cm)
Louvre Museum,
Paris

THE ASTRONOMER

The Astronomer, "twin" of *The Geographer* that was painted in 1668 and is now in the Louvre, represents the same young man depicted with long hair and dressed in an ample robe that goes to his feet, lending him the mysterious air of an exalted person. Vermeer painted the scholar seated at a desk while comparing what is in the book in front of him with the constellations represented on the celestial globe. The artist has turned the globe so that the constellation of Ursa Major is visible on the left, Hercules and Draco the Dragon at the center, and Lyra on the right, and has created an extraordinary intellectual connection between the mind and the hand as well as between culture and the senses. An expert has been able to identify the book on the desk as Adriaen Metius's *On the Investigation or Observation of the Stars*; he also discovered that the globe was made by Jodocus Hondius, a famous maker of terrestrial and celestial globes. Hondius based his globes on the work of the Danish scholar, Tycho Brahe, but then corrected them by integrating information from the navigators and mathematicians of the day. Like the geographer, the astronomer inhabits in his own small world, immersed in thought and surrounded by the tools necessary for his scientific investigations. The flat astrolabe, for example, on the table behind the rug was essential for astronomy and celestial navigation.

Once again Vermeer's scene is perfectly contextualized in the historical events and cultural debates of his time. In this case it is significant that the artist painted *The Astronomer* at the time when Louis XIV was building an observatory in Paris (1667–1672), while Isaac Newton perfected (in 1668) the reflecting telescope that had been invented five years earlier by James Gregory. Furthermore, Christian Huygens had discovered the sixth of Saturn's rings only ten years earlier.

Here the artist focuses especially on the scholar's personality, on his thought process and his eagerness for research. There are various interpretations of the work, but only one, based on the picture of Moses rescued from the Nile that hangs at the back of the room, suggests that Vermeer represented a discovery about the stars at the moment it happened. There was no clearly marked line between astronomy and astrology in the seventeenth century, and the theme of the discovery of Moses, traditionally attributed to Divine Providence, also points to other possible interpretations. Furthermore, the possibility of a semantic relationship with *The Geographer* suggests an even more articulated meaning regarding the whole of human thought. The study of the heavens (in *The Astronomer*) and of the earth (in *The Geographer*) have complicated theological implications. The first regards the kingdom of the spirit, and the other God's plans for humankind in the earthly realm. From this point of view the cartographic instruments and the maps represented in each picture can have both a scientific explanation and an allegorical meaning, representing two sides of a single coin. *The Astronomer*, who extends his hand to the celestial globe, symbolically seeks a spiritual guide, while *The Geographer*, sure that he has the proper tools to trace the course of his own life, looks toward the light. These two pictures affirm Vermeer's ability to express the idea of imagination itself in his paintings. Here the sense of mystery and an eagerness for research are depicted through the effects of a light that envelops the scholars and elevates their pursuits to the realm of the spiritual.

only two works, along with *The Procuress* (1656), that the artist dated. The first was painted in 1668 and the second from 1668 to 1669. In the seventeenth century—the Age of Discovery—the exciting exploration of unknown lands involved not only adventurers but also experts in astronomy and geography. An interest in scientific research was joined with new information brought home by explorers, and advances in cartography placed the Low Countries among the great centers for the manufacture of maps. So it is not an accident that Vermeer's *Geographer* has a new sense of energy different from the quiet and contemplative images that the artist created of women in domestic interiors—it is as if he wanted to represent the eagerness for research and discovery that distinguishes men of science. Vermeer's geographer seems stimulated by this intellectual research, and his small world comprises maps, books, and globes. The artist depicts him looking intently out the window while holding the tools of his inquiries; his left hand rests on a book and his right holds a compass. At the same time, this image does not stray from the essential enigma and ambiguity of Vermeer's work. The artist does not indicate which questions the scientist asks or the answers he seeks. Instead, he reveals the geographer's state of mind in the intense look of concentration the artist has captured. Every detail in the painting underscores the figure's intellectual endeavor, and Vermeer represents him in academic dress and with his long hair pushed back behind his ears. Moreover, the changes Vermeer made while executing the work confirm that he wanted to create a sense of energy. The compass, for example, was originally pointed down and turned more, and the scientist's head was positioned at a different angle in the first version of the composition. Even the folds of the figure's robe, which are simple but clean and carefully defined, contribute to describing an active person, and it is interesting to compare them with the textile that covers the table. The latter has a soft flow to it, a quality also found in earlier pictures, while the folds in the man's clothing are almost abstract. Through this detail in the modeling of the drapery, Vermeer tried to emphasize the dynamic aspect of the figure. As for the scientific instruments he included in the scene, they are portrayed so realistically that they can be traced to tools that were made in Vermeer's own time. The map of the world's oceans corresponds to one drawn by Willem Jansz Blaeu, and the globe mirrors one made by Jodocus Hondius in 1618. Hondius came from a family of cartographers, and Vermeer included one of the mapmaker's globes in his *Allegory of Faith*.

Those who suggest a close link between *The Geographer* and *The Astronomer* emphasize that the representation of scientific instruments in both is so sophisticated that it seems likely that Vermeer had expert help in

Opposite, with detail on the following pages:
Johannes Vermeer
The Geographer
1668–1669, oil on canvas
1.7 x 1.5 ft. (53 x 46.5 cm)
Städelsches Kunstinstitut und Städtische Galerie, Frankfurt

I Ver-Meer
MDCLXVIIII

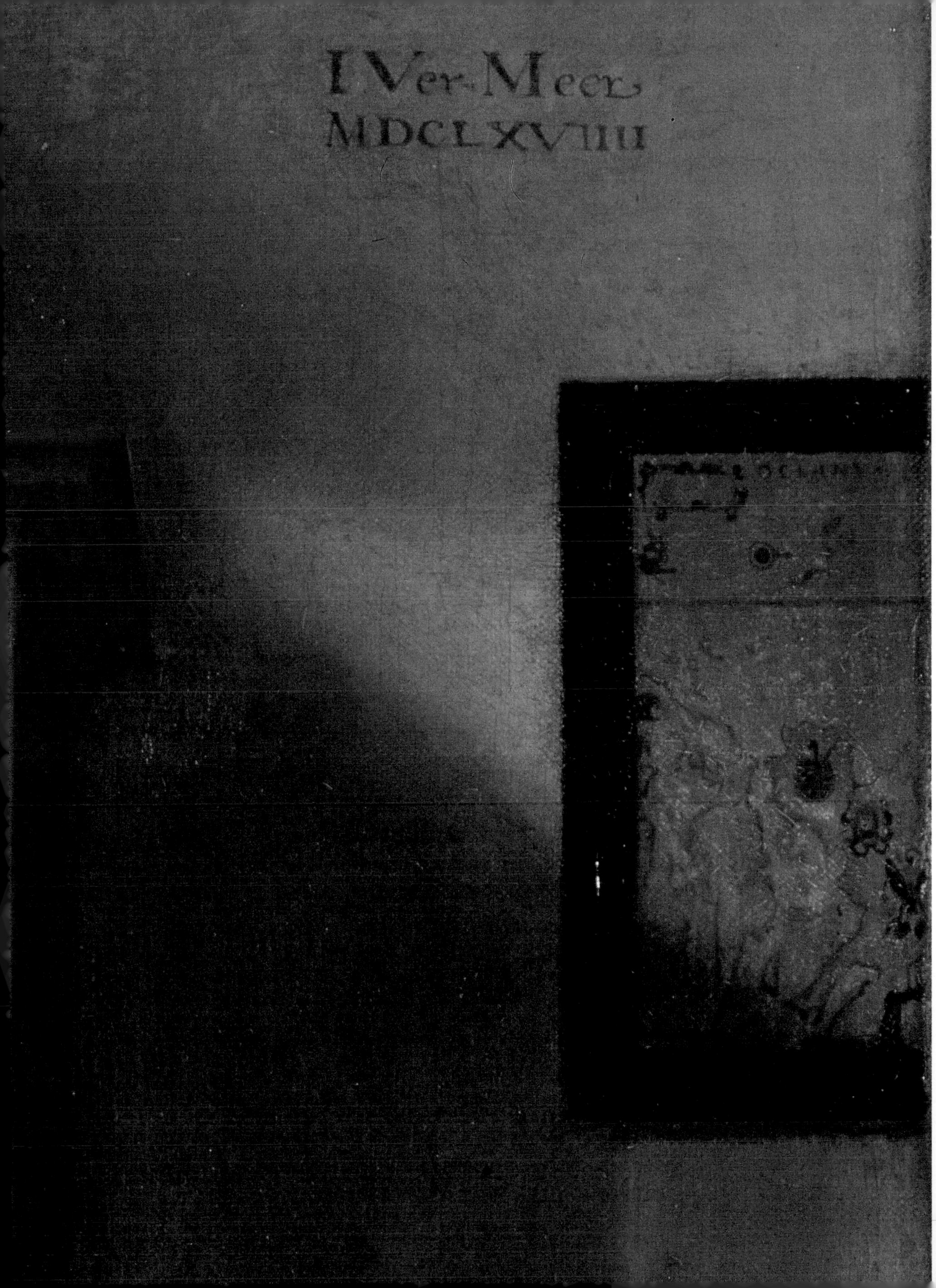
I Ver-Meer
MDCLXVIIII

painting them. Other scholars have identified the figure in the two works as a self-portrait of the artist, while others suggest that Vermeer simply used the same model in both pictures. In that case, the mysterious young man might also be the scholar who provided Vermeer with the scientific advice he needed, identified as Antonie van Leeuwenhoek, a famous naturalist and early promoter and manufacturer of microscopes who was born in Delft in the same year as Vermeer. His relationship with the artist's family is confirmed by the fact that Van Leeuwenhoek was named executor of Vermeer's estate in 1676, and it seems likely, though it is not documented, that the two men—the scientist and the painter—were friends. We know as well that Van Leeuwenhoek was also an expert in astronomy, navigation, philosophy, the natural sciences, and mathematics, and that in 1668 he would have been about the same age as the model in *The Geographer*. His friendship with Vermeer, if indeed they had one, represents a fascinating episode in the relationship between science and painting, which is not particularly surprising given the cultural climate of the period. Even if Van Leeuwenhoek did commission both *The Geographer* and *The Astronomer*, the two pictures must be considered more than simple portraits of a scientist in his study. Instead, they are images of an intense enthusiasm for research and scientific discovery. There is still some question of whether these two works were intended as pendant pieces, however, even though they were separated for the first time only after an auction in 1797.

There is some similar doubt regarding the pairing of two works executed in the early 1670s: *Young Woman Standing at a Virginal* (ca. 1670–1673, National Gallery, London) and *Young Woman Seated at a Virginal* (National Gallery, London), which is dated to more or less the same time or perhaps a little later, although some scholars date it from 1673 to 1675. Despite the fact that these works are similar in subject and format, it does seem as if they were created as separate paintings. Both are characterized by a lucidity that first appears in Vermeer's work in the second half of the 1660s, at a time when he was especially concerned with modulating tones and colors. This allowed him, in turn, to adopt a bolder and more direct technique and to substitute sharper outlines for hazier edges. His search for pictorial clarity led the artist to simplify certain aspects of his working method in order to avoid applying the paint too thickly and thus damaging the limpid quality of the image. This separates a work like *Young Woman Standing at a Virginal* from earlier pictures, in which a filtered light and fuzzy outlines contributed to emphasizing the atmosphere of quiet reflection. Now the image seems to assert itself. The young woman makes direct and determined visual contact with the viewer. Her gaze leads us to the painting of *Cupid* on the back wall

Opposite, with detail
on the following pages:
Johannes Vermeer
Young Woman Standing at a Virginal
1670–1673, oil on canvas
1.7 x 1.5 ft. (51.7 x 45.2 cm)
National Gallery,
London

of the room—his presence makes the reference to love explicit here. The virginal refers to the same amorous theme because it is traditionally associated with pure love and virginity. The same is true of the *putti* that decorate the tile baseboard at the bottom of the walls. The small, bucolic landscape next to the *Cupid*, as well as the one painted on the virginal's lid, reinforces the connection between feminine innocence and the beauty of nature. This game of references makes the woman's gaze the focal point of the composition, as it is her assertive presence that offers the invitation to contemplate and share in a harmonious and pure love. This sense of a secure moral rectitude prevailing in the scene is the result of its brightness and the harmony that characterizes the entire picture. Vermeer's stylistic movement toward cleaner forms and more directly moralizing subject matter also reflects a more general tendency among other Dutch artists of this period. Yet while an artist like Cornelis de Man introduced explicit gestures to make the meaning of his paintings unambiguous, Vermeer relied entirely on the tools of his pictorial language—color, proportion, perspective, and light—and by bringing them together he succeeded in intensifying the moral authority of his representations.

Young Woman Seated at a Virginal additionally involves the viewer by means of the figure's questioning gaze; she seems to be waiting for some comment from the person standing in front of her. The somewhat approximate manner, however, of the handling of the folds in her dress distances this work from the "abstract" quality of *Young Woman Standing at a Virginal.* Van Baburen's *Procuress* is again hanging in the room, and together with the virginal, the landscape painted on its lid, and the viola da gamba, this image plays a major role in Vermeer's picture and the interweaving of its meanings. There is the implication that someone else was in the room just moments before, suggested by the abandoned instrument in the foreground and the blue curtain drawn across the window, as if to emphasize a secret meeting hidden from the light of day. The overall sense of the picture is one of moderation, however, a feeling at odds with the suggestion of something else. Perhaps this contradiction is meant to send a more complex message than that of *Young Woman Standing at a Virginal.* There is a choice here between ideal love, represented by the virginal, which is a symbol of purity and harmony, and sensual love, recalled by Van Baburen's *Procuress* hanging behind the young woman. Light, too, plays a role to cement the theme of the picture; it highlights the three most loaded elements in the painting—the woman, who is pronounced clearly against the background, the front side of the virginal, and the viola da gamba. Music itself plays a central role in both of these works, and they allow us to admire Vermeer's masterful ability to represent different surfaces. In the second picture,

Johannes Vermeer
Young Woman Seated at a Virginal
1673–1675, oil on canvas
1.7 x 1.5 ft. (51.5 x 45.5 cm)
National Gallery,
London

the virginal and the viola da gamba are painted with almost photographic realism, which again indicates the artist's openness toward, and interest in, the culture of his own time. The precision with which Vermeer represented the detail and decoration of the musical instruments permits us to recognize them as "portraits"—just as we could with the scientific instruments. The virginals, for example, were made in Antwerp by Hans Ruckers and his successor, Jean Cuchet, and it is possible that Vermeer may have admired one in the house of Constantijn Huygens, who bought one in 1648 for 300 florins. The presence of two musical instruments in *Young Woman Seated at a Virginal* suggests, furthermore, that the picture was commissioned by Diego Duarte, a collector from Antwerp and a connoisseur of musical instruments.

The lucidity of Vermeer's execution here is demonstrated by the way he painted the floor and the tiles at the base of the walls. The different types of flooring that occasionally appear in his works have led some scholars to look more carefully at the real spaces the artist used to stage his compositions.

Johannes Vermeer
Young Woman Seated at a Virginal (detail)
1673–1675, oil on canvas
1.7 x 1.5 ft. (51.5 x 45.5 cm)
National Gallery, London

Vermeer's interest in tiles can be linked to the important business of ceramics production in Delft at that time. This industry had existed in the city since the fourteenth century, but it became especially important in the 1500s when the city began to compete with the refined porcelain being imported from East Asia. A variety of ceramics were manufactured in Delft, including the small, blue-and-white decorative tiles that became a sort of "calling card" for the middle class. This led to frequent intersections between easel painters and the artists who decorated majolica—in Vermeer's case it surfaces in his interior scenes and the faithful reproduction of the many local ceramic products they contained. It is also worth mentioning *Young Woman at a Virginal*, formerly in the Rolin Collection in Brussels, in connection with the *Young Woman Seated at a Virginal* in London. The authenticity of the former has often been questioned, yet it was sold recently at auction for a record 24.3 million euros ($31.8 million), further fueling the debate about its attribution to Vermeer.

Chapter 4
Ephemeral Splendor

There was a parallel between Vermeer's growing prosperity and the economic and social development of Delft, and the same was true of the rapid decline of both the family and the city. The painter's financial difficulties coincided with the end of the extraordinary but ephemeral splendor of his native city.

Although he did not suffer the humiliation of a public bankruptcy, as Rembrandt had, Vermeer began to feel the strain of his precarious financial situation as early as the first years of the 1660s, his difficulties caused, in part, by the slow pace at which he worked and his reluctance to enter into a binding or exclusive relationship with any one patron or dealer. Vermeer also had to deal with a less active art scene that was in turn less likely to produce commissions. Indeed, his name appears a number of times in notarial acts related to loans, suggesting that he was in financial straits, and even though he inherited Mechelen from his mother in 1670 and 148 florins from his sister in 1671, his situation did not seem to improve. Vermeer rented out the inn, but this still did not allow him to balance his accounts because of the slump in the sales of his work as well as that of the artists he represented. These circumstances worsened with the outbreak of war with France; 1672 was a catastrophic year for Holland. Louis XIV of France invaded the eastern part of the Low Countries, pushing almost as far as Amsterdam. Meanwhile, the English attacked the Dutch merchant fleet even before declaring war on Holland. William of Orange, Stadtholder of Holland and a future king of England, could not stop the enemy's advance. The only defensive tactic he could take was the extreme measure of opening the dykes and flooding a vast part of the country, a drastic decision that succeeded, however, in saving at least the western territories. The war lasted until 1674, although a final peace and the definitive redrawing of the republic's borders did not come until 1678.

Vermeer found it increasingly demanding to maintain his large family in that difficult political and economic environment, and his accumulating debt finally became unsustainable. The opening of the dykes was a terrible blow to his beleaguered finances because it flooded several farms that Maria Thins

Johannes Vermeer
Allegory of Faith (detail)
1671–1674, oil on canvas
3.7 x 2.9 ft. (114 x 89 cm)
The Metropolitan
Museum of Art,
New York

had owned in the area around Schoonhoven, which had until then provided the family with a regular income. Worse still, Vermeer was unable to sell his paintings after 1672, and this, according to his wife, brought on a health crisis that led to the artist's death in 1675.

Yet Johannes Vermeer was never better known. In May of 1672, he and an older colleague, Jacob Jordaens, who had spent many years in Italy, were called to The Hague to appraise several Italian pictures. The circumstances of the trip were this: in 1671 the dealer Gerrit Uylenburgh offered to sell twelve paintings and some statues to Frederick William, the Great Elector of Brandenburg, for the considerable sum of 300 florins. The authenticity of the paintings, however, was in doubt, and a dispute arose between the elector and the dealer that also involved the Stadtholder's secretary, Constantin Huygens, as well as many artists of the time. In the end, the final judgment on the paintings was entrusted to Vermeer and Jordaens, "eminent painters from the city of Delft." These two experts swore in front of a notary from The Hague and without hesitation that the pictures were "not only not good quality Italian paintings but on the contrary are bad pictures which are not worth even a tenth of the abovementioned prices asked for them." Unfortunately, the paintings in question were not listed separately, so it is impossible to judge Vermeer's competency as an art expert. The episode does attest, however, to the great reputation the artist enjoyed even as a connoisseur of foreign pictures, a status likely gained through his father's activity as an art dealer in Delft.

Vermeer seems to have been very busy in the last two years of his life, at least judging from the many times he is mentioned in notarial acts and other documents. He was also active in the civic guard in Delft at that time, and this brought him into contact with important officials. Some of them—like Pieter Claesz van Ruijven, with whom Vermeer had a close relationship—also had large art collections. From 1674 on the only documentary evidence we have of Vermeer comes in regard to his duties as administrator of property belonging to Maria Thins and his wife. Of his many children, only his daughter Maria achieved financial independence before his death—she was engaged to Johannes Gillisz Cramer, the son of a well-to-do silk merchant, on May 26, 1674. They were married shortly afterward in Schipluy.

Joseph Parrocel
Louis XIV's Army Crossing the Rhine
1699
Louvre Museum, Paris

The scientist Antonie van Leeuwenhoek, already associated with the paintings of *The Geographer* and *The Astronomer*, played an important role in the events that preceded and followed Vermeer's death. The friendship between them may also have been driven by greater interests because Van Leeuwenhoek manufactured scientific instruments, including the first microscopes built with an ingenious system of mounted, compound lenses. Vermeer's relationship with this inventor, who had introduced a continual flow of innovations in the field of optics, may have inspired the artist's interest in using a camera obscura to help him paint his interior scenes—his last paintings offer evidence of a skilled ability to reproduce the optical effects of the act of seeing, perhaps using an instrument that allowed him to focus on details not visible under normal conditions. In truth, the question of whether Vermeer made use of a camera obscura is still much debated; there is no firm documentation to prove it, but it is nevertheless possible to argue that he did based only on the characteristics of those late paintings.

Among the artist's later works, *The Lace Maker* (Louvre Museum, Paris), a small picture painted between 1669 and 1670, is filled with passages of extraordinary effects of light and color that suggest the possible use of optical tools, followed by a series of modifications made in transposing the image to the canvas. Recent studies have revealed that Vermeer's knowledge of perspective came primarily from studying the manuals that circulated in his time, in addition to his connections with cartographers, considered the true source for the "art of measuring," or geometry; Antonie van Leeuwenhoek, who had a degree in cartography from Delft, was probably among the most competent of them.

We can, by looking carefully at some of Vermeer's pictures, reconstruct the method he used to create the perspective of his interior space. There are physical traces revealing that the artist stuck a pin through the vanishing point on his prepared canvases to then attach a string that could reach to all areas of the painting. He used the string to create perfect orthogonal rules, that is, the straight lines that converge at the central vanishing point. Vermeer dipped the string in gesso and then probably stretched it tight, with the pin in one hand while snapping the string with the other so that it hit the canvas surface. This left on

Jan Verkolje
(Engraved by Abraham de Blois)
Portrait of Antonie van Leeuwenhoek
1723
Gemeentearchief, Delft

Opposite, with detail
on the following pages:
Johannes Vermeer
The Lace Maker
1669–1670, oil on canvas
9.4 x 8.3 in. (24 x 21 cm)
Louvre Museum,
Paris

THE LACE MAKER

One of Vermeer's masterpieces, *The Lace Maker* (painted between 1669 and 1670 and now at the Louvre) is generally counted among the three paintings described as *exempla virtuti*, or models of virtue; the others include *Woman with a Water Pitcher* and *The Kitchen Maid*. This small work is also one of Vermeer's most famous paintings, with the single figure of a young lace maker dominating the canvas. Intent on her task, she is seated behind a table with a blue embroidery cushion set on top of it. Perhaps more here than in other works, the boundary between reality and the image is almost invisible. This is achieved by both the size of the painting and the immediacy of the figure, which is placed very close to the picture plane; these two factors serve to focus the viewer's attention entirely on the lace maker. Gazing at her additionally leads to understanding how hard she is concentrating, which is underscored by her lowered gaze and physical characteristics that communicate something of her state of mind: the severity of her coiffure set with soft curls that fall almost rhythmically toward her shoulders, her posture, and her yellow dress—an active and psychologically intense color. The viewer's desire to come as close as possible to the figure is manipulated by Vermeer's optical techniques, which make the objects closest to the viewer appear less focused than those further away. This happens, for example, with the colored threads that come out of the cushion and the floral motif of the tablecloth, both painted with almost liquid brushstrokes. The same pointillist technique is used to render the woman's work tools—the needles stuck into the cushion and the wooden spools of thread—and to soften the lace collar of her dress. In so doing, the artist creates different depths of field, as if the viewer is truly standing in front of a three-dimensional scene. The most imprecise forms in the foreground force the viewer's gaze back to the better-focused middle ground, where the lace maker herself is located. As he does in all his works, Vermeer creates a perfect relationship between the mind, the hand, and the work, painting optical and pictorial effects appropriate to the meaning of what he is depicting. The difference in focus between the objects in the foreground and the lace maker suggests that her activity is extraneous to her surroundings, and thus that she is enclosed in her own, almost independent dimension. In the same way, the significance of her concentration is absolute as well. In light of the virtue of domesticity, she also has a religious meaning akin to Solomon's *Proverbs*, which says, in part, "A virtuous woman ... seeketh wool and flax ... she layeth her hands to the distaff, and her hands hold the spindle."

The little book Vermeer painted on the table next to the woman is almost certainly a book of prayers or a small Bible. It functions to emphasize the moral character of the scene. Beyond any specific references to religious precepts, however, the virtue celebrated here is the attention she pays to her work, an activity that requires special concentration and involves creative abilities.

The lack of focus in the foreground suggests that Vermeer observed the scene through a camera obscura, so that he could reproduce the optical effect of seeing the scene in his painted image, although he certainly did not project the image directly on the canvas and then paint it. His absolute mastery of light and color is the only tool Vermeer needed to achieve the miraculous effects of optical realism in the small but intense picture of *The Lace Maker*.

the prepared surface gesso lines that were reinforced with a brush or pencil to trace the perspective system of the scene. At the time this technique was more common among painters of architectural scenes, but the fact that Vermeer used it in at least some of his pictures is confirmed by the pinhole left on the surface of each canvas. Vermeer's likely reliance on a camera obscura in *The Lace Maker* should not be seen as overly systematic, however, given that this tool did not serve so much for tracing the initial drawing as it did to help him achieve the optical effects he wanted through the use of color. A pin and a piece of string were all he really needed to make images with absolutely correct perspective; he created the rigorous illusion of space for an almost abstract composition in order that it might allow for the "revelation of the universal in the everyday."

Productive in his mature period, *The Guitar Player* (ca. 1671–1672, Iveagh Bequest, English Heritage, Kenwood), in addition to *The Lace Maker*, reaffirms Vermeer's interest in continuing his pictorial research. This painting is listed as belonging to the artist's widow in the inventory of 1676 because she had given it to the baker, Hendrick van Buyten—perhaps also with *Lady Writing a Letter with Her Maid* (*The Letter*), now in Dublin at the National Gallery of Ireland and dated only a little earlier, ca. 1670—in payment for an outstanding debt. The musical instrument in *The Guitar Player*, like the lute, induces the soul to amorous daydreams. The guitar is juxtaposed to a number of single objects placed in the dark, shadowy corner of the room. The instrument and the pastoral landscape hanging on the wall both refer to love, although on the whole this scene seems to suggest that the lovers can only remain hidden in their dark room like the shepherds of Arcadia, which are nothing if not a memory. Vermeer was already a master of color and light when he began this picture, and he worked across the canvas with extreme skill. The girl, caught in a brief moment of intimacy as she picks out chords on her guitar, is no longer lost in her own musings but is seen, instead, communicating with the outside world.

The other work that eventually came to belong to the baker, *Lady Writing a Letter with Her Maid*, is another example of how well Vermeer could pack universal meaning into the apparent banality of everyday life. He could do this because when he painted he was very careful to avoid anything anecdotal or that referred to specific situations. In this picture, also known as *The Letter*, the artist eliminated nearly all superfluous objects and used light, color, and perspective to reinforce a sense of the timelessness of the moment being represented. Simplicity is the organizing element in the scene. A seated woman writes a letter in a large and austerely elegant room. The other woman in the room, her servant, is standing quietly with her head turned toward the window. There is no communication between the two women and no hint of the subtle complicity between figures that characterized some of Vermeer's earlier works

Opposite, with detail on the following pages:
Johannes Vermeer
The Guitar Player
ca. 1671–1672, oil on canvas
1.7 x 1.5 ft. (53 x 46.3 cm)
Iveagh Bequest, English Heritage, Kenwood

depicting similar subjects. Everything here is peaceful, without a trace of any movement or unexpected event. Of the scene an important scholar of Dutch painting wrote that "the tranquility inside the room radiates with a peacefulness humanity cannot seem to find within itself." Vermeer's muted colors and an emphasis on the lines that structure the space create a subdued atmosphere in which the women's different positions suggest a precise psychological meaning. The maid, standing, is possessed of an almost statuary calm, and her central position—she is aligned with the vertical edge of the picture frame behind her—gives her a certain dignity, while the regular and well-defined drapery folds in her dress accentuate the sense of stability and steadfastness she emanates. Her mistress instead leans off center on her left elbow, suggesting a lively and emotional intensity that is amplified by the tight space between her and the right border of the painting. His precise use of light allowed Vermeer to highlight the almost angular rhythm of the folds in her clothing, which helps create a sense of interior tension. The artist's genius is apparent in using the expedient of perspective to relate these two figures. The orthogonal lines that begin at the upper and lower edges of the window follow the maid's bent arm and converge at the vanishing point in the seated lady's left eye. This encourages the viewer's gaze to move across the painting until arriving at the thematic center of the composition. Without needing to create a narrative context to reveal what the seated figure is thinking, Vermeer succeeds in presenting an intimate drama by means of his pictorial technique and the symbolic elements in his work. Among the most important of these are the large painting on the wall, which represents *The Finding of Moses* (and which we have already seen in *The Astronomer*), and the crumpled letter on the floor, its importance indicated by Vermeer's tendency to eliminate all unnecessary accessories. Because the religious theme of the picture within the picture can refer to Divine Providence or God's ability to bring peace to warring parties, some experts have related it to the torn-up letter and the standing servant. These three elements might refer, symbolically, to inner peace, which was understood as reconciliation and considered obtainable through personal strength and faith in God, which in turn leads us to serenity of the humble maidservant.

One of Vermeer's last works, the *Allegory of Faith* (ca. 1671–1674, The Metropolitan Museum of Art, New York) stands apart from the rest of the artist's oeuvre because it is so clearly an allegory, and thus akin to the *Allegory of Painting*. Herman van Swoll's catalogue for the 1699 sale in Amsterdam describes the painting as a "seated woman invested with a variety of meanings tied to the New Testament, by Vermeer of Delft and painted with energy and fervor." The asking price was 400 florins, perhaps because it was a large

Opposite, with detail
on the following pages:
Johannes Vermeer
Lady Writing a Letter with Her Maid (The Letter)
ca. 1670, oil on canvas
2.3 x 2 ft. (71.1 x 60.5 cm)
National Gallery
of Ireland, Dublin

painting, its execution extraordinary, and the subject considered "difficult." Van Swoll was the painting's first owner, and he seems to be one of the few people who succeeded in obtaining a work by Vermeer before the 1696 auction. The commission for the work is not documented, although scholars associate it with the Jesuit community in Delft or perhaps some rich and devout Catholic patron.

The *Allegory of Faith* remains true to the artist's earlier visual language (a domestic interior in which the "realness" of the objects is tangible and concrete) but at the same time reveals the allegorical nature of the scene, using the multicolored curtain pulled aside to the left to introduce the viewer into "another" space beyond the real world, just as he did in his *Allegory of Painting*. Once again, Vermeer turned to Cesare Ripa's *Iconologia* to help him choose the symbolic elements he needed in this work, although he also made many changes to the descriptions in the text. Ripa described four allegories of faith, and although some of them share a few of the attributes of the figure in the painting, none corresponds to it exactly. Vermeer's personification of Faith is an elegantly dressed woman in a blue-and-white satin dress trimmed with gold. She is seated on a raised, rug-covered platform. One foot rests on a globe, her right hand clasps at her breast, and her gaze is transfixed by the glass sphere hanging from the ceiling above her. A screen of worked leather has been placed before the rear wall, behind a table bearing a crucifix, an open bible, and a gold chalice. The elements introduced here by Vermeer that did not come from Ripa are the crucifix, the globe, and the large painting of the *Crucifixion* on the rear wall, a reproduction of a work by Jacob Jordaens owned by Maria Thins, which is listed in the 1676 inventory of her property. Again the artist enhanced the significance of the scene by introducing a "picture within a picture," offering a revised iconography that sometimes mixed its sources and sometimes followed them to the letter. For example, Ripa says that "Faith has the world at its feet," so Vermeer put a real globe under the woman's foot. At the same time, the crucifix, which stands out against the reddish screen behind it, gives the painting a Eucharistic significance absent in Ripa's *Iconologia*. The suggestion of possible Jesuit patronage is supported by the central position of the representation of Christ's sacrifice, and by the fact that a domestic interior was chosen for this scene, possibly playing on the Jesuits' belief in the importance of praying in the intimacy of one's own home. Whoever the patron may have been, it was Vermeer who decided which objects to include in the scene and where to place them. He was certainly aware that, unlike his earlier paintings, this work demanded the viewer's attention—and assumed a greater ability to decipher its complicated iconography. The abstract ideas in his other pictures were expressed by representing human situations

Johannes Vermeer
Allegory of Faith
1671–1674, oil on canvas
3.7 x 2.9 ft. (114 x 89 cm)
The Metropolitan
Museum of Art,
New York

and concrete objects, and thus the viewer could at least understand their real appearance and could appreciate them even without fully understanding their more profound significance. The *Allegory of Faith* does not allow this, especially because some of its iconographical elements—including the woman's ecstatic pose and the snake crushed by a rock that symbolizes evil defeated by Christ—would not have been very familiar to a typical Dutch Protestant audience. It is also true that the combination of theological ideas with domestic realism can be read as an attempt to combine biblical material with ordinary people by setting the scene in an ordinary space. It has also been noted, however, that Vermeer did not and could not here ignore the trend toward the courtly, classical painting style that was spreading in Amsterdam and Leyden at this time if he wanted to be free of the restraints imposed on him by the cultural isolation of his final years.

Vermeer's financial problems were the major concern in the last year of his life. On March 26, 1675, he was in Gouda to renew the lease on land his mother-in-law had inherited from her late husband. In July he was in Amsterdam seeking a 1,000 florin loan from Jacob Rombouts, a local merchant. There are few other references to him in the documents available until he died, on December 13 or 14, 1675. The cause of his death remains unknown, but a year and a half later his widow, Catharina, described his dramatic demise in testimony before the assembly of the states of Holland and West Frisia when she petitioned it to allow her to use income from Diewertje van Hensbeeck's trust to support her children: "During the long and ruinous war with France not only was he unable to sell any of his paintings, but to his detriment, he was also not able to sell works by the other artists he represented. As a result, and also because of the large responsibility of raising his children without enough means, he fell into such ruin and decline and suffered to such a point that he fell into a delirium, so that in the course of a day or a day and a half he passed from a healthy man to death." From this testimony we can infer that Vermeer, worn out by his economic difficulties and desperate because he could not support his family or pay his debts, had a heart attack and died only a couple of days later. He was buried on December 15 in the family tomb in the *Oude Kerk*, the Old Church, in Delft. The entry for that day in the books of the Camer van Charitate, the municipal charity department, notes "nothing to take out," meaning that there was nothing in the customary box that had been sent to the house of the deceased so that his heirs might make a donation to the poor. The Vermeer family donated nothing; they could not, because their budget had been reduced to a bare minimum. Catharina found herself with eleven children to feed, of whom ten were still minors, and her situation soon became untenable. In January 1676, the widow was constrained

Johannes Vermeer
Allegory of Faith (detail)
1671–1674, oil on canvas
3.7 x 2.9 ft. (114 x 89 cm)
The Metropolitan Museum of Art, New York

to sell two of her husband's last works to settle the considerable debt he owed to baker Hendrick van Buyten. On February 10, she sold twenty-six canvases to art dealer Jan Coelenbier for a paltry 500 florins, permitting her to settle another of her husband's debts. Vermeer's widow had only one of her husband's works left, the *Allegory of Painting (The Artist's Studio)*, but shortly afterward she was forced to cede it to her mother, who called in a loan she had made to her son-in-law. In the meantime Vermeer's property was inventoried and then divided up between his wife and mother-in-law. In April Catharina was forced to go twice to the high court at The Hague to demonstrate that she could not pay her debts and to ask for custody of her husband's property. In particular she asked for and received letters of assignment that deferred payment on her debts. At the same time she received a judgment that required her mother to return the *Allegory of Painting*, a work she seemed unwilling to part with. The following year, on September 30, the city councilors of Delft nominated the scientist Antonie van Leeuwenhoek as trustee in bankruptcy and executor for Catharina, who was trying to retrieve the twenty-six paintings she had sold to Jan Coelenbier. Some scholars have questioned just how friendly the relationship was between Van Leeuwenhoek and the Vermeer family, suggesting that if Maria Thins and her daughter had been free to choose their own trustee, they would have preferred a Catholic to a Protestant, and that any real bonds of friendship would not have allowed Van Leeuwenhoek to make decisions (as he did) not in their best interest. Maria Thins had contested the judgment against her, and the *Allegory of Painting* was not included in the public auction that Van Leeuwenhoek ordered in February 1677 to sell the twenty-six paintings. She was not successful in her appeal, however, and the picture was finally put on sale on March 15 along with what remained of Vermeer's property. Catharina and her mother petitioned the magistrates of Gouda again in 1678 to help in the dire situation of the children, two of whom were gravely ill. Maria Thins died two years later, on December 27, 1680, and she was buried near Vermeer in the tomb of the Old Church. Her daughter died on December 30, 1687, but she was buried in the New Church.

If Vermeer's children and grandchildren were quickly forgotten, his work remained famous after his death among contemporary collectors. Two of the most important of them, the baker Van Buyten and Jacob Abrahamsz Dissius, kept the works they owned by Vermeer until they died. Furthermore, the paintings sold at the auctions of 1696 and 1699 went for very good prices.

The first of these sales is especially important in reconstructing Vermeer's career because it reconnects him to his principal patron, Pieter Claesz van Ruijven. In 1696 the Dissius collection was sent from Delft to

Johannes Vermeer
Allegory of Painting (The Artist's Studio)
(detail)
1666–1667, oil on canvas
4 x 3.3 ft. (120 x 100 cm)
Kunsthistorisches Museum, Vienna

Amsterdam to be sold at auction, and it included the largest single group of Vermeer's paintings put up for sale to date. Of the 134 total paintings offered, 21 were by the painter from Delft. Dealer Gerard Honet organized the event, and the announcement in the *Amsterdamsche Courant* stated that the auction would include "a variety of paintings and works of art including twenty-one splendid works painted with great skill by J. Vermeer of Delft. They are of different compositions, the best he ever made." The auction catalogue and prices were published in the nineteenth century by Théophile Thoré-Bürger, one of the central figures in the modern rediscovery of Vermeer. The remarkable number of Vermeer's works offered in the 1696 sale led to the longstanding belief that their owner, the printer Jacob Dissius, was the artist's principal patron. Recent studies have demonstrated, however, that his real patron was Van Ruijven, Dissius's father-in-law. Dissius himself inherited the collection from his wife, Magdalena van Ruijven, in 1682. Over the course of time, Van Ruijven's original collection of Vermeer's pictures was added to by its new owners until it comprised the twenty-one works auctioned off after Dissius died in 1695. The question of the relationship between the artist and Van Ruijven remains controversial, however. The most recent research suggests that it is likely that Van Ruijven acquired some of the pictures sold at the Dissius auction shortly after they were painted, from 1650 to 1660. The research further suggests that he was in continuous contact with the painter at this time. From 1660 to 1665 Van Ruijven acquired other pictures, including *The Kitchen Maid*, *The Concert*, and the *View of Delft*.

The 1696 auction testifies to Vermeer's fame, especially because, for the most part, it attracted real art enthusiasts. One Isaac Rooleeuw stands out among the buyers. He purchased *Woman Holding a Balance* for 155 florins and *The Kitchen Maid* for 175 florins; the latter was considered the most important of Vermeer's works in the sale. An unknown collector acquired the *View of Delft* for 200 florins. Shortly afterward Rooleeuw declared bankruptcy, and Vermeer's two canvases passed into the hands of Paulo van Uchelen, a prominent bibliophile. The pictures were separated when Van Uchelen's estate was distributed among his heirs after his death. Others who collected Vermeer's work include Herman van Swoll, director of the Amsterdam branch of the Hamburg postal service and the first owner of the *Allegory of Faith*, and Diego Duarte, a rich jeweler and banker in Antwerp, who probably owned *Woman Standing at a Virginal* or *Woman Seated at a Virginal*. These sales reveal that Vermeer's work was sought after in the years immediately following his death. Nonetheless, the artist's name and his fame were both forgotten soon thereafter. This led to mistaken attributions of his works as early as the

Johannes Vermeer
The Concert
1664–1666
oil on canvas
2.3 x 2 ft. (69.2 x 62.8 cm)
Isabella Stewart
Gardner Museum,
Boston (stolen in 1990)

eighteenth century, when paintings by Vermeer were identified as by Pieter de Hooch and Gabriel Metsu.

The career of one of the greatest protagonists of seventeenth-century Dutch painting ended as it had begun, with few documentary references and little evidence of its existence. Modern scholars still argue about the exact number of pictures Vermeer painted over the course of his life. A lack of documentation complicates this question, as does disagreement among the experts on attributions based entirely on stylistic analysis. The number of autograph works varies between thirty-five and forty-five; eight more are mentioned in seventeenth-century inventories but have been lost, and about thirteen survive but without any documentation. Based on the two most commonly accepted theories, it appears that the painter from Delft executed a total of somewhere between forty-six and seventy paintings, including those that were lost.

Chapter 5
Obscurity and Immortality

Although he was well known and his work appreciated in his lifetime, Vermeer was forgotten soon afterward and not rediscovered as one of the truly great seventeenth-century Dutch artists until the middle of the nineteenth century. The painter was so closely tied to his hometown of Delft that when it fell into decline, the memory of the painter followed suit.

The pall that fell over Vermeer's reputation was probably also due to the change in taste among collectors and dealers in Holland, who, by the beginning of the eighteenth century, seemed bored by tranquil scenes of "good times past." They were more interested in the "refined French style" as well as the prevailing monumental manner used to represent literary and mythological subjects at the time. A dearth of Vermeer's work in the marketplace may have further contributed to obscuring his memory, as the largest group of his paintings was dispersed among various collectors after the 1696 auction.

Vermeer's name and his fame may have been lost to time, but his pictures remained much sought after among art lovers and experts. This sustained interest also meant that his paintings continued to rise in value. As early as the seventeenth century, however, they were mistakenly attributed to a variety of other masters—although they were always recognized as Dutch and considered valuable. Pieter de Hooch, Frans van Mieris, and Gabriel Metsu are among the names attached to pictures by the painter from Delft, and one of the first mistaken attributions identified *The Music Lesson* as a work by Van Mieris. It was acquired by King George III of England in 1762 as part of the collection of John Smith, the British consul in Venice, who had bought it for a few *soldi* from Angela Carriera, widow of the painter Gianantonio Pellegrini. It seems likely that this painting was part of the group sold at auction in 1696, and the numerous times it changed hands is only one example of the dispersion of Vermeer's works. Many collectors, including those outside Holland, recognized the quality of his works, but because the painter's name had been forgotten they were attributed to other artists of his time.

Johannes Vermeer
View of Delft (detail)
1660–1661, oil on canvas
3.2 x 3.9 ft. (98.5 x 118.5 cm)
Mauritshuis,
The Hague

The *Groote Schouburgh*, the most important lexicon of Dutch art in the eighteenth century, was written by Arnold Houbraken and published in

Amsterdam in 1718 to 1721. It offers proof that Vermeer's recognition had already largely disappeared not long after his death: his name does not appear in its lists of important artists, and this oversight also explains why nothing was published about the painter in all of the eighteenth century. In 1792 the art dealer Jean-Baptiste-Pierre Lebrun underscored the scarce attention scholars paid to Vermeer, "This Van der Meer, about whom the historians say absolutely nothing, deserves particular attention. He was a great painter in the mold of Metsu. His works are rare and are better known and appreciated in Holland than anywhere else." The situation began to change only after the French Revolution, when several paintings by the "Master of Delft" began to leave Dutch collections and appear in auction houses and galleries in Paris. Several of Vermeer's pictures from collections in Flanders, Switzerland, Holland, and Italy were sold at auction in the French capital in 1811. As Lebrun wrote in the sale catalogue, "This skilled observer of the most intimate essence of nature was also capable of rendering it with great bravura." The consul Smith published a catalogue of the "most eminent" Dutch painters in 1833, and this time Vermeer was included. He was described as a pupil and follower of Metsu and De Hooch. Interest in the artist continued to grow, focusing largely on the unknown artist's extraordinary use of color. In 1857 Maxime Du Camp wrote this about the *View of Delft*, in the *Revue de Paris*: "Except for the sky, which is soft and fluffy, the work is painted with a vigor, a solidity, and a firmness of paint that is rare in Dutch landscapes. This Jan Van der Meer, whom I only know by name, was a vigorous painter who used flat colors, broadly applied in overlaying layers. He must have visited Italy. He is an exaggerated Canaletto."

It is not accidental that Vermeer was rediscovered in France, where his work resonated with the values of the rapidly expanding middle class in the 1850s. The bourgeoisie saw their "artistic" redemption in the Dutch painter's calm interior scenes, read as mirrors of a domestic reality with similar social and economic characteristics to those in France at that time. Vermeer's rediscovery also came in a period when French critics and the public began to see a strong similarity between his work and that of the Impressionists. The latter group of artists had emphasized the value of light and color and used loose brushstrokes to achieve a greater luminosity in their paintings, offering these works as an alternative to the Academic style that they believed was no longer capable of representing the spirit of the modern age. In this sense Vermeer was identified as a "forerunner" of the period, an artist who used the potential of light and chromatic intensity so powerfully in his work that he broke new ground. The Impressionists' aesthetic revolution needed a father figure, and Vermeer fit the bill. Modern painters transformed his detached subject matter and quest for fixed, immobile scenes built on a relationship between space, light, and color

into their images of crowded Parisian boulevards. Vermeer proved himself an artist capable of showing the world as it had never been seen, the world we all think we know, but which, in reality, still has some unknown essence of itself to offer.

The definitive rediscovery of Vermeer is usually credited to Étienne-Joseph-Théophile Thoré, a socialist politician and critic better known by his pseudonym, William Bürger, a name he adopted for political reasons. He brought the artist to international attention in the *Gazette des Beaux-Arts* in 1866. His articles reintroduced Vermeer into the history of art, even if the nickname he coined for the artist, the "Sphinx of Delft," in reality masked a wealth of information about his life. Thoré-Bürger was responsible for recognizing Vermeer's style and personality, and for correcting the attributions of several of his works previously assigned to other masters.

The *View of Delft* was the first painting to call widespread attention to Vermeer. It was acquired by the Mauritshuis in The Hague at the insistence of King William I, his interest piqued, perhaps, because William the Silent, "father of the nation," was assassinated and buried in Delft. The first three articles that Thoré-Bürger dedicated to Vermeer developed earlier observations he had made upon seeing the painting in The Hague, a work he considered, as early as 1842, "a superb landscape and rather unusual" that "attracts the attention of all visitors." Perhaps it is closer to the fact, then, to say that the real first rediscovery of Vermeer was made by King William I and his art consultant, the British consul John Smith. Their interest was then followed in due course by that of a series of critics and scholars, among whom Thoré-Bürger was probably the most important. He conducted research of the collections in Berlin, Brussels, Brunswick, Dresden, Vienna, and, of course, The Hague, re-attributing works to Vermeer that he found in a variety of European collections and encouraging many of his admirers to buy these pictures. For this reason Thoré-Bürger was seen, as early as 1860, as the real force behind the re-evaluation of the artist from Delft. He also noted the stylistic particularities in Vermeer's work that tied the painter to the theory of "color as luminous feeling" that was popular in artists' circles in the middle of the nineteenth century. Some of the observations

Gabriel Metsu
Woman Embroidering
1650s
Pushkin Museum,
Moscow

Thoré-Bürger made in 1866 remain telling observations: "Light in Vermeer is not at all artificial; it is precise, normal, and as it is in nature, just like a scrupulous physicist would want it... The precision of Vermeer's light also comes from the harmony of his colors."

A sort of pointillist technique allowed Vermeer to leave the foreground in his paintings unfocused—an effect observable with a camera obscura—and it gave his work an abstract quality. It was this quality in his pictures that attracted the most attention from modern critics and, beginning in the 1830s, spurred his growing fame. Vermeer's work became the third inimitable example, alongside that of Rembrandt and Frans Hals, of Dutch painting in its "golden century." Critic recognized this, but so did contemporary artists who believed that color and light were the vital elements in their own works. Van Gogh, for example, wrote to Émile Bernard, in about 1887 to 1888, "Do you know an artist called Jan van der Meer? He painted a lovely and very distinguished Dutch lady who is pregnant. This strange artist's palette includes blue, lemon yellow, pearl grey, black and white. It is true that one can find the whole range of colors in the pictures he painted; but the combination of lemon yellow, a dull blue, and light grey is as characteristic in his work as Velazquez's combinations of black, white, grey, and pink ... The Dutch had no imagination, but they did have extraordinary taste and an infallible sense of composition." Camille Pissarro, too, was fascinated by the artist from Delft, writing in 1882 to his son Lucien that he could not help but wonder "how to describe these portraits by Rembrandt and Hals, or the view of Delft by Vermeer, masterpieces so close to the works of the Impressionists."

Vermeer was much discussed at the end of the nineteenth and the beginning of the twentieth century, and many amazing similarities with contemporary painting were found in his work. At the same time a careful search for any information that might throw light on this largely unknown personality continued. Inevitably, some artists were more especially susceptible to the fascination of Vermeer's works than others. The masterful Pierre Bonnard, a member of the Nabis, is one example. *The Letter*, a picture he painted in 1906 and which is now at the National Gallery of Art in Washington, D.C., is a

Above:
Rembrandt van Rijn
Self-portrait
1669
Mauritshuis,
The Hague

Opposite:
Frans Hals
Jester with Lute
1624–1626
Louvre Museum,
Paris

reworking of the delicate intimacy of *The Lace Maker* as well as in perfect harmony with the predominant Western artistic spirit at the beginning of the twentieth century. The "Sphinx of Delft" was also the focus of some memorable competitions among American collectors who paid mind-boggling figures to have his best work. The first Vermeer to cross the ocean was *Young Woman with a Water Pitcher*, which was given to the newly founded Metropolitan Museum of Art in New York by Henry G. Marquand in 1889. It was followed by *The Concert*, which Isabella Stewart Gardner personally purchased at the auction of the Thoré-Bürger collection in 1892. She became immediately known in the international art market as a ferocious competitor, pitting herself as the principal rival of the equally seasoned Pierpont Morgan. Unlike Gardner, however, Morgan was not up to date on the latest publications documenting the rediscovery of the Dutch painter, making the phrase "the name of the great Dutch painter was unknown to Morgan" famous. Yet when the antiquarian Hellman showed him *Mistress and Maid*, Morgan immediately recognized the quality of the painting—and was fully prepared to pay $100,000 to have it. The passion the great American collectors developed for Vermeer guaranteed that the artist quickly became a "best seller." This is clear in another astonishing sale; in 1928 Abraham Bredius, director of the Mauritshuis, sold the *Allegory of Faith* to an enthusiastic American collector for $300,000.

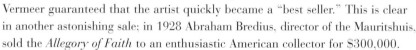

Vermeer's fame was officially consecrated in 1935 by a large exhibition in Rotterdam called Vermeer: Origins and Influences. According to the catalogue, "Together with Rembrandt, Vermeer rises above all the other artists in the great school that was the seventeenth century." In truth the image the show offered of the artist was not accurate because six of the paintings exhibited in it were not by Vermeer. The ability to attribute works to the Dutch master accurately had not yet been achieved, and this explains how clever forgers were able to fool even the most famous and experienced connoisseurs. Hans van Meegeren offers the best example. At the end of the 1930s he took full advantage of the scanty knowledge experts had about Vermeer, especially regarding his youthful works of sacred subjects. He offered several of his own pictures for sale, forgeries that

were inspired by Vermeer's early works. Van Meegeren was clever enough to study the smallest details of Vermeer's technique, and this made his forgeries credible. He used old canvas, old looms, and old nails taken from minor seventeenth-century works and imitated Vermeer's technique in order to understand the qualities of his pigments, to fool well-known art historians. One of Van Meegeren's greatest successes was *The Supper at Emmaus* (Museum Boymans van Beuningen, Rotterdam), which he painted between 1936 and 1937. Based on favorable reports by the museum's director, Abraham Bredius, and the critic Dirk Hanema, the museum in Rotterdam acquired the forgery in 1938 for 100,000 florins. Other works signed by Vermeer also circulated; they were considered undisputed examples of the artist's early style, and no one expressed any doubt about their authenticity. Yet the scheme Van Meegeren had built so carefully was destined to collapse, and by his own hand. In May 1945 American soldiers of the Seventh Army found a *Christ and the Adulterous Woman* signed by Vermeer along with other artworks hidden by the Germans. An investigation revealed that it had been purchased in Amsterdam for an exorbitant price on behalf of the Nazi minister Hermann Goering; Goering's contacts led to Van Meegeren. He was arrested, and to avoid being accused of collaboration he confessed to having executed the *Christ and the Adulterous Woman* between 1935 and 1943, along with other canvases that were believed to be autograph works by Vermeer. The Dutch tribunal charged with trying him decided to test the forger, forcing him to paint a picture while they watched. Although the court was incredulous, it was clear that he had been telling the truth. Van Meegeren died in prison a year later, in 1946, leaving behind a legacy of tremendous confusion among both academics and antiquarians.

The publication of numerous monographs on Vermeer followed this extraordinary incident, including those by Pieter T.A. Swillens, Sir Lawrence Gowing, Vitale Bloch, and Ludwig Goldscheider, although the most complete reconstruction of the artist's career was not made until the publication of Albert Blankert's study in 1975. The critical literature had, as early as 1946, highlighted only the most interesting aspects of the important work by the artist from Delft.

Vincent van Gogh
Still Life with Pears
1888–1889
Gemäldegalerie,
Dresden

"Vermeer unwound domestic subjects, portraits, landscapes, and even, early in his career, mythological and religious works. He brought something to them that was entirely new and unique in the seventeenth century, and that was the revelation of the platonic idea of painting in and of itself," according to Antony Blum. He then emphasized the perfect union Vermeer created between art, nature, and ideas. Within the context of seventeenth-century culture and in the realm of genre painting, where everything was anecdotal and frivolous, the master of Delft created a dialogue between poetry and rationality to reveal a sense of the eternal hidden behind everyday appearances, toward which he still maintained a certain distance. As André Malraux wrote in *Les voix du silence* ("The Voices of Silence") in 1951, "His anecdotes are not anecdotes, his atmospheres are not atmospheres, his sentiments are not sentimental, his settings are just barely settings ... He seems always to mask the character of his models, making the universal synthetic to obtain not types but a sensitive abstraction which reminds us of some Greek *korai*."

The fascination of Vermeer's art attracted the greats of modern literature as well as art lovers. Proust paid the artist his greatest compliment when he wrote a moving passage about Vermeer after he saw an exhibition of Dutch painting at the Jeu de Paume Museum in Paris in May 1921. On that occasion the writer had the opportunity to admire the *View of Delft*, and it led him to make some changes to his famous and already completed novel, *Remembrance of Things Past*. He added a scene to volume five, called *The Captive*, in which an observation of Vermeer's *View of Delft* precedes the death of the writer Bergotte. Wrote Proust:

> At last he came to the Vermeer which he remembered as more striking, more different from anything else he knew, but in which, thanks to the critic's article, he noticed for the first time some small figures in blue, that the sand was pink, and, finally, the precious substance of the tiny patch of yellow wall. His dizziness increased; he fixed his gaze, like a child upon a yellow butterfly that it wants to catch, on the precious patch of wall. "That's how I ought to have written," he said. "My last books are too dry, I ought to have gone over them with a few layers of colour, made my language precious in itself, like this little patch of yellow wall."

Camille Pissarro
Landscape at Pontoise
ca. 1872
Musée d'Orsay,
Paris

And so Vermeer became a dramatic element in the novel. The Italian specialist in French studies, Giovanni Macchia, noted that the artist was "the impassive catalyst of one of the loveliest episodes," that is, the death of Bergotte. This episode in Proust's novel is a complicated one, and it raises a series of questions. The most enigmatic regards the "little patch of yellow wall" that captured most of Proust-Bergotte's attention—but which, in truth, does not appear in the View of Delft, causing many scholars to wonder about this "error" by the writer. The mistake, in the end, is best thought of as "artistic imprecision" on Proust's part, which came about from his taking in more than one detail in the *View of Delft* with his eyes and later reconstructing it in his mind as a single image. Vermeer's little patch of wall became Proust's, a detail of the Dutch landscape that existed only on the writer's page. Proust and Vermeer were united by a shared affinity that led them to extol stillness, silence, and listening to silence as moments when the most secret of essences might be revealed. Vermeer's painting became a symbol of Proust's search that was made possible through the exercise of memory, and an appreciation for Vermeer also appears in other passages in the novel; he is Swann's favorite artist, because he reflects the state of mind that the character himself was seeking. The pursuit of introspection in Proustian memory requires an attenuated concentration assisted by stopping the passage of time. The seventeenth-century Dutch master accomplished the latter so skillfully on his canvases that Proust's connection with Vermeer—he had considered the painter his favorite artist since he was twenty—ignited the writer's need to return constantly to the same museums where he had already admired Vermeer's works, to gaze at them again and again while discovering new mysteries in the images.

If Proust represents an example of a precious bequest from that master of Dutch painting to one of the great masters of literature, then we can say the same about a great master of the cinema. The German Wim Wenders was one of the leading directors in the second half of the twentieth century, with works including *Paris, Texas* and *Wings of Desire*, among other great films. Wenders often took inspiration for his films from such great figurative artists as Friedrich and Hopper as well as Vermeer, about whom the director said, "[B]ut for a cinematographer there is no one but Vermeer. He is the only one who gives you the idea his pictures might begin to move. He would be the supreme camera man." Wenders thought of Vermeer as a cinematographer because the light in his paintings was like a character in a movie, which acted to immobilize figures and landscapes in a moment of concentrated suspension. And Wenders' films certainly have frames inspired by Vermeer. The angle of the shot is thus essential, and so are the composition and the

formal equilibrium necessary to eliminate the accidental and to realize a completely controlled reality. The artist behaved, in fact, much like a director in constructing his interior scenes, framing his images in a way that was itself a vehicle for profound feeling. Wenders knew how to borrow this aspect of Vermeer's work with an unparalleled sensitivity. Scenes from *Paris, Texas*, for example, recall details from the *Allegory of Painting*, the intervening centuries magically melting away.

The notion of Vermeer as a painter "suspended in time" was recently the basis of another interesting intersection of literature and cinema, this time based on Tracy Chevalier's novel *Girl with a Pearl Earring*, a fascinating reconstruction of Vermeer's personality and of his small world in seventeenth-century Delft. Based on fact and historical probability and constructed from a careful study of seventeenth-century Holland as well as the artist's own biography, Chevalier introduced just enough fantasy to make the atmosphere around Vermeer and his family more magical. Through the character of Griet, identified in the novel as the model who posed for the mysterious portrait that gave the book its title, we can enter the private and otherwise inaccessible world of the painter's studio, where nothing could be moved, even to clean, so as not to risk any slight change in the appearance of the settings for his masterpieces. As we read, we sense the atmosphere of suspension that hovers in the paintings, we hear the same silence, and understand its beauty and uniqueness. The success of the novel reaffirmed the greatness of a painter who is too often confined to a time—the seventeenth century—that is seen as distant from our contemporary world, but which, in reality, is much closer than we think. The film followed shortly after the publication of the novel, and it attracted the same public that had already been fascinated by the book and wanted to match a face to the mysterious artist in their own imaginations.

Is it true that the "Sphinx of Delft" kept a secret that can never be revealed? No one can say, but perhaps the enigma of Vermeer's art is simply its power to reveal, in silent contemplation of the ordinary people and things around us, the timeless truth in each of our small, personal universes.

Pierre Bonnard
Woman with Dog
Musée Toulouse-Lautrec, Albi

Index

Page numbers in *italics* indicate illustrations. All works are by Vermeer unless otherwise indicated.

Further Reading

Bailey, Anthony. *Vermeer: A View of Delft*. New York: Owl Books, 2002.

Chevalier, Tracy. *Girl with a Pearl Earring*. New York: Dutton, 2000.

Gaskell, Ivan and Michiel Jonker, eds. *Vermeer Studies (Studies in the History of Art Series)*. Washington, DC: National Gallery Washington, 1998.

Liedtke, Walter, et al. *Vermeer and the Delft School*. New York: Metropolitan Museum of Art, 2001.

Montias, John Michael. *Vermeer and His Milieu*. Princeton, NJ: Princeton University Press, 1991.

Wheelock, Arthur K. *Johannes Vermeer*. New Haven, CT: Yale University Press, 1995.

———. *Vermeer: The Complete Works*. New York: Harry N. Abrams, 1997.

Wolf, Bryan Jay. *Vermeer and the Invention of Seeing*. Chicago: University of Chicago Press, 2001.

Image Credits

The illustrations in this volume were supplied by the Scala Archive, the most prestigious fine art archive in the world. The more than 60,000 subjects are accessible through a computerized system that permits easy, quick iconographic research of any degree of complexity. Website: *www.scalarchives.it*; e-mail: *archivio@scalagroup.it*. Other images supplied by:

p. 2 Vienna, Kunsthistorisches Museum
p. 4 Dresden, Gemäldegalerie, Photo: Artothek
p. 17 Vermeer, Jan (Johannes), called Vermeer van Delft; 1632–1675. "Saint Praxedis", 1655. Oil on canvas, 101.6 x 82.6 cm. The Barbara Piasecka Johnson Collection. Photo: akg-images.
pp. 19, 20-21 Edinburgh, National Gallery of Scotland
pp. 24-25, 26-27 Dresden, Gemäldegalerie, Photo: Artothek
pp. 28-29, 30-31, 32-33 New York, The Metropolitan Museum of Art, Bequest of Benjamin Altman, Photo: ©1995 The Metropolitan Museum of Art
pp. 34-35, 36-37 New York, © The Frick Collection
pp. 39, 40-41, 42-43 Dresden, Gemäldegalerie, Photo: Artothek
p. 44 The Metropolitan Museum of Art, Marquand Collection, Photo: ©1993 The Metropolitan Museum of Art
pp. 51, 52-53 Braunschweig, Herzog Anton Ulrich-Museum
pp. 54-55, 56-57 Berlin, Staatliche Museen zu Berlin, Gemäldegalerie, Photo: BPK
pp. 59, 60-61, 62-63 Amsterdam, Rijksmuseum
pp. 64-65, 66-67 New York, The Metropolitan Museum of Art, Marquand Collection, Photo: ©1993 The Metropolitan Museum of Art
pp. 68-69 Berlin, Staatliche Museen zu Berlin, Gemäldegalerie, Photo: BPK
pp. 71, 72-73, 74-75 Washington, National Gallery of Art, Widener Collection
pp. 77, 78-79 L'Aia, Mauritshuis Foundation
pp. 81, 82-83, 86 Amsterdam, Rijksmuseum
p. 87 London, © National Gallery
pp. 88-89 Amsterdam, Rijksmuseum
pp. 90-91, 92-93 L'Aia, Mauritshuis, Royal Cabinet of Paintings
p. 95 New York, The Metropolitan Museum of Art, Gift of Mr and Mrs Charles Wrightsman, Photo: ©1979 The Metropolitan Museum of Art
p. 96 Washington, National Gallery of Art, Andrew W. Mellon Collection, © Board of Trustees, National Gallery of Art, Washington
pp. 98-99 Washington, National Gallery of Art, Widener Collection
pp. 100-101 London, Buckingham Palace, The Royal Collection © 2004, Her Majesty Queen Elizabeth II
pp. 102-103, 104-105 Boston, Isabella Stewart Gardner Museum
pp. 106-107 New York, © The Frick Collection
pp. 108-109 New York, The Metropolitan Museum of Art, Bequest of Collins P. Huntington, Photo: © 1995 The Metropolitan Museum of Art
p. 110 Vienna, Kunsthistorisches Museum
pp. 113, 114-115 Washington, National Gallery of Art, Gift of Harry Waldron Havemayer and Horace Havemayer
pp. 116-117, 118-119, 120-121 New York, © The Frick Collection
pp. 122-123, 124-125, 126-127 Amsterdam, Rijksmuseum
pp. 129, 130-131, 132-133 Vienna, Kunsthistorisches Museum
pp. 135, 137, 138-139 Paris, Louvre, Photo: RMN
pp. 141, 142-143 Francoforte, Städelsches Kunstinstitut, Photo: Artothek
pp. 145, 146-147, 149, 150-151 Londra, © National Gallery
p. 152 New York, The Metropolitan Museum of Art, The Friedsam Collection, Bequest of Michael Friedsam, Photograph © 1994 The Metropolitan Museum of Art
pp. 157, 158-159 Paris, Louvre, Photo: RMN
pp. 161, 162-163 Kenwood, The Iveagh Bequest, © English Heritage Photo Library
pp. 165, 166-167 National Gallery of Ireland, Photo: Courtesy of the National Gallery of Ireland
pp. 169, 171 New York, The Metropolitan Museum of Art, The Friedsam Collection, Bequest of Michael Friedsam, Photo: ©1994 The Metropolitan Museum of Art
pp. 172-173 Vienna, Kunsthistorisches Museum
pp. 174-175 Boston, Isabella Stewart Gardner Museum
p. 176 L'Aia, Mauritshuis, Royal Cabinet of Paintings

This 2007 edition published by Barnes & Noble, Inc.

Translated by Lawrence Jenkens

ISBN-13: 978-0-7607-8959-9
ISBN-10: 0-7607-8959-2

Printed and bound in China

1 3 5 7 9 10 8 6 4 2